LOCAL GOVERNMENT
in
SCOTLAND

LOCAL GOVERNMENT
in
SCOTLAND

THIRD EDITION

By

GEORGE MONIES
Former Lecturer, Napier University

W. GREEN/Sweet & Maxwell
EDINBURGH
1996

First published 1985
Second edition 1989
Third edition 1996

© 1996
W. GREEN & SON LTD

ISBN 0 414 01059 0

A catalogue record for this book is
available from the British Library

The moral rights of the author have been asserted.

Typeset by LBJ Enterprises Ltd, Aldermaston
Printed by Redwood Books Limited, Wiltshire

FOREWORD

The first edition of this important book was published in 1985 and described the structure and procedures of local government in Scotland after the reorganisation of 1975 resulting from the Wheatley Report. The second edition in 1989 saw substantial revision dealing with legislation in the late 1970s and 1980s which changed the relationship between central and local government. This third edition has been substantially rewritten to deal with the consequences of the recent government decision to revert to all-purpose one tier local authorities in Scotland.

The author is uniquely well placed to make this contribution to our understanding of local government. For many years he taught politics and government at Napier University. From 1974 to 1984 I knew him as a valued colleague on the City of Edinburgh District Council. During this period we had first hand experience of some of the changes described in the first two editions of this book. I am sure this third edition will help students and others to understand the new local government system.

Dr John McKay
Lord Provost of Edinburgh, 1984–88

PREFACE

The second edition of this book commented that the powers of local government had been reduced so much that there might be no need for a third edition. However, the major reconstruction of the local government system brought about by the 1994 Act has necessitated this new edition.

As with the previous editions the purpose has been to reach students and interested onlookers and, once again, makes no pretence to be a technical or academic study—there are now a considerable amount of books dealing with these aspects of local government.

The author would like to thank friends, councillors and officials who have contributed their advice and knowledge but with special thanks to John McKay and John Mulvey and also the various editors at W. Green. Because of the continued changes in local government it was felt that a bibliography would soon be out of date and thus is omitted but the author would like to recognise the help provided by the Annotated Acts of Scotland published by W. Green. Any errors are, of course, the responsibility of the author. With the likelihood of some form of devolved government to Scotland in the near future perhaps, on this occasion, there will be need for a fourth edition.

The author would like to dedicate the book to Helen and Paul Monies and his mother Sarah Monies.

Edinburgh
February 1996   G.M.

CONTENTS

CHAPTER 1

THE SEARCH FOR A SYSTEM

Local government has a long history in Scotland but it was only in the nineteenth century that a structure was developed. Inevitably the structure had to be changed to meet changing circumstances. The first major rationalisation of local government was in the 1890s; some minor changes were made after the First World War but it was felt necessary to restructure the system in the mid-1920s. The Local Government (Scotland) Act 1929 was the first comprehensive local government Act in Scotland but the changes made then proved not to be sufficient to cope with the large-scale problems after 1945.

Major changes in central government policies in the 1940s and 1950s brought criticism about the local government system and many local authorities found it difficult to carry out their statutory duties. The need for reform was recognised by the 1960s but opinion was divided on what structural changes were required to take the local government system into the last quarter of the twentieth century. It was for this reason that Royal Commissions were set up in 1966 and the Wheatley Report of 1969 proposed a radical reorganisation of local government in Scotland.

Most of the recommendations of the Wheatley Report were enacted in the Local Government (Scotland) Act 1973 and subsequent legislation. Successive governments since then have attempted to tidy up the system. The Conservative governments elected since 1979 have, however, redefined the role of local government. This redefinition has led to a variety of legislation affecting the powers, functions and management of local government in Scotland. These changes were so extensive that the Government decided, after the 1992 election, that the structure and powers of local government should be, yet again, reorganised. This new structure came into effect in 1996.

1

The Burgh System

The core which ran through local government and administration in Scotland until 1975 was the burgh. The first burghs were established by David I in the twelfth century. The purpose of the burgh was twofold. In the absence of any effective method of controlling the country, *i.e.* a legal system and an army, the Crown established garrisons in strategic positions. In return for protection the burgh was given a monopoly of foreign and local trade. The Crown extracted revenue from this granting of monopoly, some of which was used for the upkeep of the garrison. Therefore law and order and trade were the initial responsibilities of the burghs.

Apart from the burghs, local affairs like education and poor relief were the responsibilities of kirk sessions after 1560. The cost of education and poor relief was met by the heritors or landowners in each parish. Some of the wealthier landowners were nominated "commissioners of supply" by the Crown which meant that they were responsible for collecting revenues. Each county also had "justices of the peace" who were responsible for public order and the maintenance of the highways.

In the landward areas, the powers of the commissioners of supply were extended. In addition to law and order and roads they were given control of the militia, authority for levying rates, control of police, registration of electors and appointment of valuation assessors. From 1889 to 1894 local government in the landward areas was reformed and by the end of the century Scottish local government consisted of:

County councils	33
Burgh councils	200
Parish councils	869

There were numerous other authorities including burgh police commissioners, county road boards, county district committees, burgh and parochial school boards.

After the First World War there was further rationalisation of local government. About 1,000 school boards were replaced by directly elected education authorities numbering 38. These were often referred to as ad hoc education authorities. In 1929 a major reform of local government took place. The Local Government (Scotland) Act 1929 abolished many councils, committees and various burghs. Burghs were reclassified as either large burghs (having a population over 20,000) and small burghs (having a population over 2,000). County councils and counties of cities (a new classification) became education authorities replacing the ad hoc education authorities. In the landward areas of counties certain local services became the responsibility of district councils. The 1929 system therefore consisted of:

Counties of cities (all-purpose)	4
County councils	33
Large burghs	21
Small burghs	171
District councils	196

Apart from the four cities the 1929 system could be described as a four-tier system.

Post-War Problems

The reorganisation of 1929 was no doubt intended to last for many years, but no one could have predicted the events of the next 25 years. The 1930s saw massive unemployment which created strains on the social services, many of them still the responsibility of local authorities. The Second World War again altered the role of local authorities. The central government took extensive economic, financial and social powers and the local authorities became mere agents of central government.

With changes in the range, nature and scale of local authority functions after 1945 there also came increased central government control of local authority decision-making. The trend in central government administration was towards greater economic and social planning. These administrative controls through general Acts like the Local Government (Scotland) Act 1947 and specific Acts like the Education Acts had required local authorities to conform to certain minimum standards laid down by central government and also to seek approval from the Secretary of State for Scotland for a host of other actions. To statutory and administrative controls were added financial controls.

This brief description of the development of local government in Scotland brings out two main features. First, with the growth of local services the small local authority found it increasingly difficult to survive. Thus we saw, with each reform, the disappearance of parish councils, school boards and eventually, in the 1970s, the small and large burghs.

Secondly, the ever-increasing involvement of central government, particularly in the fields of economic and social planning, meant that local authorities were dealing more and more with central government and often under the close supervision of central government departments.

The general direction of local government, therefore, was always towards larger units, and central government was a party to encouraging this, because it felt that larger units would mean more efficient local government. However, as many were to argue, larger units meant less democratic local government. It was this problem which the Wheatley Commission attempted to solve between 1966 and 1969.

The Wheatley Report

The Royal Commission on Local Government in Scotland was set up in May 1966 under the chairmanship of Lord Wheatley, and published its report in 1969. The commission interpreted its terms of reference as excluding consideration of administrative or legislative devolution and new methods of finance for local government. In hindsight such exclusions may seem glaring in the light of later developments. The commission, however, felt that it could consider the transfer of functions from central government or other agencies to local government and that there was no specific limit to its consideration of the size or scale of local government units. The commission's approach was to analyse the then existing local government system and to lay down certain basic objectives for a reformed or reorganised system.

The 1973 Act

Although the Wheatley Report had been largely accepted by a Labour Government, it fell to the subsequent Conservative Government to enact the proposals. Between a White Paper in 1971 and the passing of the Local Government (Scotland) Act 1973 there were many changes. In particular there was a change of emphasis away from the regional predominance of the Wheatley Report to a more evenly divided two-tier system. In addition a new category of council was created for Orkney, Shetland and the Western Isles which were given "most-purpose" responsibilities. The final result of these changes was to produce a structure of nine regional councils, 53 district councils and the three islands councils.

The 1973 Act created a structure of 65 local authorities from a system which had contained over 400 authorities. Leaving aside the islands councils it was a two-tier system. But it was a tier system of functions, not of authority, except in the planning sector. In other words each tier was assigned a set of functions which were thought appropriate to that type of authority. Thus the "big" local authorities' functions were assigned to the regions. These included education, social work, transportation, police, fire, and water and sewerage. The districts were assigned housing, recreation, environmental services and district courts. Islands councils were most- (not all-)purpose authorities but some services were assigned to neighbouring regional authorities. The planning function was given to all authorities but, again, with certain exceptions as will be explained later.

The above description of assigned functions sounds simple but it was more complicated. It has to be remembered that the regional authorities ranged in size from Strathclyde, with half the population of Scotland, to Borders Region with a population of 105,000 which was less than the population served by Dundee District Council. For historical and practical reasons certain district functions in the "rural" regions were assigned to the regions. For example, before 1975, public libraries in many rural areas were housed in schools. Libraries were a district function while schools were a regional function. It was therefore decided that libraries in those districts within Highland, Dumfries and Galloway and Borders regions should be a regional function. It has been noted that the islands councils were most-purpose authorities but these authorities were too small to carry out certain functions like police, water, sewerage and valuation and were amalgamated with the neighbouring region for these purposes.

Of all the functions planning was the most complicated. The Wheatley Report had recommended that this be a "concurrent" function, i.e. shared by both district and region, and made a distinction, fashionable at the time, between local and structural planning. Structural planning was assigned to the regions and local planning to the districts. However most rural district councils could not afford to maintain a planning department and gave up their responsibilities to the regions. This happened in Highlands, Borders and Dumfries and

Galloway regions where local planning committees composed of both district and regional councillors were set up.

It can be seen from the above description of functions that the system was not clear cut and that local exceptions had to be made to deal with local circumstances. The changes which were made from the Wheatley Report to the 1973 system were largely due to political factors rather than any administrative philosophy. The Wheatley Commission had not been unanimous in its recommendations and a minority viewpoint was also published. This had criticised the "big authority" solution of the majority report and suggested smaller and, therefore, more authorities. During the period from the Labour White Paper in 1969 to the passing of the Act in 1973 there had been considerable changes. The Conservatives had favoured a better balance of responsibilities between regions and districts. This was not just an administrative view.

Many Conservatives, knowing that the bigger regions would be Labour controlled, were determined to trim the regional powers. Wheatley had recommended that housing be a regional function but the Conservatives moved housing from the regions to the districts. Wheatley had recommended seven regions and 37 districts the Act specified nine regions, 53 districts and the three islands authorities. During the passage of the Bill there were some strange cross party alliances, for instance, to create a Fife Region and to reduce the size of the projected Greater Glasgow District Council. Thus the ultimate reform was arguably the result not of a rational approach to reform but a series of political compromises passed by a Conservative government which did not have a majority in Scotland.

The new authorities took over from the old authorities in May 1975 after one year of "parallel" government. Even up to the last day of the old system there had been attempts to delay the implementation of the new system. Many were dismayed at the abolition of the old burghs which were perceived as the bedrock of Scottish local government. It was felt that the new authorities were too big and would not be in touch with their electors. There was particular criticism of the vast Strathclyde Region with a population of two and a half million and stretching from south Ayrshire to the Inner Hebrides.

Despite the fact that it had been a Conservative Government that had passed the 1973 Act most of the criticisms in the early years came from Conservatives. This may not have been unrelated to the fact that the bigger local authorities were all Labour controlled. Nevertheless after the return of the Conservatives in 1979 a committee was set up to inquire into the concurrent functions of regional and district councils. This committee was chaired by Mr Alex Stodart, a former Conservative MP and Minister of State at the Scottish Office. The committee reported in 1981 and its main proposals did not suggest any major alteration of the structure of the new system. The main aim of the report was to "tidy up" overlapping areas between regions and districts. Interestingly for later developments the report rejected the idea of all- or most-purpose authorities and also rejected the argument about creating most-purpose status for the four city districts.

The Stodart recommendations resulted in the Local Government and Planning (Scotland) Act 1982 which re-allocated some functions between districts and regions. Recreation and leisure had been a concurrent function in the 1973 Act but the Conservatives saw this as unnecessary overlapping and gave all responsibilities in this area to the districts. Other responsibilities like countryside matters, nature conservation and tourism were also given to the districts although regions still had some say in these areas. District councils were also given sole responsibility to assist community councils. Other changes to the 1973 Act relating to planning and rating were also made. As can be seen the direction of changes was from the regions to the districts in keeping with Conservative attitudes. These were to be the first of many changes to the 1973 system.

After the 1983 election the Conservative approach to the role of local government became more radical. There were two reasons for this. First, many Labour local authorities, mostly in England but also in Scotland, began to be controlled by left-wing radicals and some by the so-called "militant tendency". These authorities had led the fight against local authority financial restrictions imposed by the Conservatives (the latest in a series of attempts to curb local authorities over the years). Conservative determination to control radical Labour authorities led, in England, to the abolition of the bigger authorities like the Greater London Council in 1986. Conservative action in Scotland was mainly aimed at Lothian Region and what had been the Conservatives' "jewel in the crown", Edinburgh District Council, which had, for the first time in its history, become Labour controlled.

Secondly, local government was to become part of the general political philosophy of privatisation. It was argued by the Conservatives that big spending and inefficiency went together, thus the necessity of spending curbs. Inefficiency was to be reduced by the introduction of service tendering. This meant that some local authority services, or part of its services, traditionally done "in house" were to be put out to tender. The Local Government Act 1988 compelled local authorities gradually to dismantle their direct services and put contracts out to tender, albeit that the local authority "in house" section could also tender for the contract. This process was to lead over the years to local authorities being less and less providers of services and more and more enablers of services on the American model.

Perhaps the best examples of this development can be seen in the two major local authority functions—housing and education. Although sale of council houses had existed under Labour governments, after 1979 legislation made it compulsory for authorities to sell to tenants and to offer large discounts. This naturally led to a reduction of the number of council houses, especially since there were now restrictions on the building of new council houses. Thus district council responsibility for housing decreased. In addition the maintenance of council houses had usually been done "in house" by the housing or maintenance department. Under legislation enacted in 1980 this responsibility had to be put out to tender. Education in Scotland has always been largely a local authority responsibility. However the Self-Governing Schools etc. (Scotland) Act 1989 allowed school boards to vote for self-governing status and effectively take them out of local authority control. We shall consider this later.

Thus by the early 1990s the functions and powers of local authorities in Scotland had been radically changed and reduced. Later chapters in this book will detail these developments in each of the services but Conservative reform of local government did not stop at functions and powers. Although there was little evidence of corruption in local government the government decided that standards amongst councillors and officials were falling. A committee was set up—the Widdicombe Committee—to look into this matter and report. This inquiry into the internal management of local authorities resulted in the Local Government and Housing Act 1989. This Act limited the powers of councillors in terms of the committee system, appointment of officials, council standing orders, councillors' conditions and payments. Such inter-ference in the internal workings of local authorities was seen by many as unwarranted, unnecessary and, possibly, undemocratic. Thus by the beginning of the 1990s the nature and purpose of the 1973 system had been changed radically by "creeping" reform. One other change was to disrupt local government more than all the others.

It was to be in the area of finance that the most changes were made. The spending cuts brought in by Labour and Conservative governments since the mid-1970s had met with considerable opposition. By the mid-1980s these restrictions on finance meant that most Scottish local authorities only directly controlled about 20 per cent of their income, the remainder coming from general and specific grants controlled by the Scottish Office. This 20 per cent came from domestic and business rates which, despite various attempts to control these by central government, were decided by local author-ities. During the 1987 election the Conservatives had prom-ised that they would abolish the rating system without proposing any specific alternative. After the election the Government announced that the domestic rating system would be abolished and replaced by a new local tax called the community charge and that the business rate would be decided, not by local authorities, but by central government.

Conservative thinking about local revenue raising was that the rating system had too narrow a base, ratepayers being only a proportion, estimated at 20 per cent, of local electors. To the Conservatives this meant that local councils could put up rates knowing that those who paid were only a minority of voters. Many local authorities had increased rates in order to cover spending cuts. Since the community charge was to be levied on all adults then local authorities would act more responsibly and now be accountable to all electors.

The implementation of the community charge, known to most people as the poll tax, in Scotland in 1989 was to be an administrative and political disaster. Even Conservatives later were to accept that the reform was misguided. The campaign against the tax was so effective that when it was replaced in 1993 by the council tax Scottish local authorities were still owed millions of pounds (estimated at £550 million in 1995) on unpaid bills. Thus before the 1992 election the 1973 local government system had been subjected to considerable change and disruption.

Recognising this the Scottish Office produced a consulta-tion document in 1991—*The Structure of Local Government in*

Scotland; The Case for Change/Principles of the New System. This caused some resentment in Scotland because there was to be a full-scale review of local government in England, including public participation, but in Scotland the Scottish Office was to orchestrate the changes. In other words, it was argued, the Government had already made up its mind about the shape of reform and the public were simply to respond to this.

The 1991 consultation document argued that the two tier system was confusing to the public; that it led to duplication and inefficiency; and that there was friction and delay between authorities. It may be noted here that there was very little evidence produced to support these criticisms. It was certainly true that many functions and responsibilities of local government had been lost or reduced and this suggested that the scale of local government did not justify the size of some of the authorities, particularly the larger regions. The opposition parties in Scotland, with an eye to a future Scottish parliament, accepted that a two tier system was, perhaps, unnecessary but were suspicious of the Government's motives. Smaller local authorities would mean more control by the Scottish Office and since the bigger councils were Labour controlled it was assumed that by breaking these up it would reduce Labour control of local government.

Another document—*The Structure of Local Government in Scotland: Shaping the New Councils*—was published in 1992. It was a detailed consideration of the proposed new structure. There were four maps illustrating alternative structures composed of either 15, 24, 35 or 51 units, together with an estimate of the cost of reform. There was considerable controversy about whether there would be costs or savings involved. This document was followed, in 1993, by a White Paper—*Shaping the Future–The New Councils*—which outlined a structure of 28 councils, including the three islands councils which were largely unaffected. It was proposed that the new "shadow" councils should be elected in 1995 and take executive powers in April 1996. The White Paper also discussed other subjects concerning functions, finance and internal management which will be discussed in the appropriate chapters which follow.

After this White Paper there was considerable public discussion although some local authorities refused to co-operate with the machinery of reform and instructed their officials to have nothing to do with it. Nevertheless the legislation went through Parliament with little controversy although changes were made. The end result was that there were to be 29 new unitary authorities to replace the regional and district authorities on the Scottish "mainland" together with the three islands authorities. Such controversy as there was was focused on boundaries and the number of councillors.

Although there were some boundary changes these were nothing like the changes which had occurred during the passage of the 1973 Act. As to councillors it would seem that the Government got hoist with its own petard. Having argued that local government must be brought closer to the people it had to concede, when faced with the arguments, that one way of doing this was to have more councillors in each local authority. During discussions with the Government the number of wards (and therefore councillors) increased. Some of the new authorities did well. For example Borders, Fife and Dumfries and Galloway councils doubled the number of councillors from the Government's proposals. The 1973 system had had 1,695 councillors while the system introduced by the 1994 Act was to have 1,245. The implications of this small reduction in the number of councillors will be discussed later in Chapter 7.

Throughout the reform process the opposition parties in Scotland had always been suspicious of the Government's motives. It was charged that they were reforming local government and changing boundaries not for the good of local government but in order to gain some electoral advantage in an area where the Conservatives were weak. If this was the intention of the Conservatives then they made a serious political error. The elections to the new unitary councils took place on April 6, 1995. It has often been said that local government elections are more to do with national politics than with local politics. These elections proved the point. The Conservatives, nationally, were at a very low ebb and the election results illustrated this. Of the 1161 seats up for election (there were no elections in the islands councils) the Labour Party won 613, the SNP 181, the Liberal Democrats 123 and the Conservatives 81. The remainder were won by declared Independents. No council was controlled by the Conservatives.

CHAPTER 2

LOCAL AUTHORITY FUNCTIONS

Despite the fact that the new system abolished *all* regional and district councils and replaced them with the new authorities, some of them have the same boundaries.

The new system abolished district councils in the Highlands, Fife, the Borders and Dumfries and Galloway. The functions of these district councils were transferred to the new unitary authorities which have the same boundaries as the former regional councils. It is difficult to understand the Government's view that this was bringing local government closer to the people in those areas. Only in the former Grampian, Tayside, Central, Lothian and Strathclyde regions were the regional functions transferred to unitary (smaller) authorities. In addition, the old regional names in these areas survive for police and fire responsibilities. Once again it is difficult to understand the Government's view that the system introduced by the 1973 Act was confusing when, for instance, Glasgow City Council will now perform most responsibilities, but people will have to deal with Strathclyde Police, the Mid and South Western fire service, and Strathclyde Transport. Further, for everyone in Scotland, water and sewerage services will be provided by the East, North and West water and sewerage authorities.

The following description of local authority functions is not intended to be exhaustive—that requires a book on its own. It is, however, intended to give a broad picture of the main functions. Since all local government functions are legally under the supervision of specific government departments we shall indicate the role of these government departments. Finally, since local authorities co-ordinate their activities through the Convention of Scottish Local Authorities (COSLA) we shall look at the role and influence of that organisation.

Education

Both in terms of people involved and money expended, education is the biggest single service provided by local authorities in Scotland. It would be easy to assume that education is mainly concerned with children but education authorities provide a wide range of educational services for all ages. Perhaps the easiest division of education is into compulsory and non-compulsory.

Compulsory education in Scotland takes place between the ages of five and 16 years. Local authorities are obliged by statute to provide a place at an educational establishment for all children in their area who are of school age. In addition to this the education authority is obliged to satisfy itself that school-age children who do not attend local authority schools are attending a recognised school or are receiving "adequate tuition".

In return for providing education for school-age children the local authority receives a grant (through the Revenue Support Grant) from central government. Since education accounts for 45 per cent of the RSG, naturally the Secretary of State for Scotland, through the Scottish Education Department, has taken considerable supervisory powers over this service. Most of these powers are concerned with the laying down of standards and cover such items as qualifications of staff, class sizes, school organisation, standards of accommodation, school terms, school closures, catchment areas, etc.

Until 1981 local education authorities had the discretion to draw up school catchment areas. This meant that all school-age children in a particular area attended the designated school for that area. Some exceptions were made by the education committee for individual cases, *e.g.* partially handicapped children. These catchment areas were often drawn so as to achieve a satisfactory "social mix". However since 1981 there has existed the "Parents' Charter".

This allows parents to send their children to the school of their choice. Local authorities can still draw up catchment areas but parents are not obliged to send their children to the designated school. One consequence of reorganisation has been that local authority boundaries may now run through a previous (regional) catchment area. The 1994 Act compels a local authority to pay the cost of a child attending another local authority school otherwise there may have been disruption to the child's education.

The School Boards (Scotland) Act 1988 requires local education authorities to set up school boards. The composition and powers of these boards vary from area to area and this will be discussed later. However, following on this legislation, the Self-Governing Schools etc. (Scotland) Act 1989 allows these boards to decide if they wish to "opt-out" of the local authority sector and be financed directly by the Scottish Education Department. To date only two schools in Scotland have voted to opt-out.

As an example of increasing central government control of the Scottish Education Department we may cite some recent developments. Mirroring the introduction of the National Curriculum in England and Wales the Government produced the 5–14 Development Programme, which schools have to offer. Within this was also implemented "national testing" at the ages of seven, 11 and 14. This caused considerable controversy when started. Teachers, particularly in Strathclyde, refused to administer the tests and many parents boycotted the tests by not sending their children to school on test days. The Government was forced to delay implementation and to lengthen the implementation period. There have been changes too at the fourth, fifth and sixth years. In the fourth year students sit the Standard Grade which is offered at three levels while in the fifth and sixth years students do Highers and Advanced Highers (replacing the Certificate of Sixth Years Studies). All these examinations are set by the Scottish Examination Board. Since 1992 there has also existed the HM Inspectorate of Audit whose duty is to collect, analyse and publish information on the performance of schools. This has been called the "league table" of schools and has been much criticised.

Other changes decided upon by the Scottish Education Department include teacher assessment, school handbooks and school development plans. The Government argues for these on the basis of improving the quality of education and extending choice. Although all those wishing to teach in Scotland must have degrees and have undergone a recognised teacher training course they now have to undergo assessment of their work every two years. The idea of the school handbook is to give to parents as much information as possible about the school. These handbooks are required to give information on school policy, school costs, attendance and absence records and, for secondary schools, results of public examinations. In addition education authorities must give parents of primary seven pupils tables comparing the secondary schools in their area. From 1995–96 schools have had to produce a school development plan setting out the school's plans and targets. There are other requirements to be fulfilled which will be discussed in the section on School Boards.

The non-compulsory sector of local authority educational provision is very diverse. Pre-school provision is often referred to as nursery education but a complicating factor here is that there are two departments (and committees) involved in this. The education department is normally involved in providing nursery classes for those over three years old—these take place in the normal school hours and are the responsibility of a qualified teacher. These nursery classes are often in the same building as the primary school, thus ensuring a smooth transition from non-compulsory to compulsory education. The Government is proposing a voucher scheme for nursery education to try to provide a nursery place for all four-year-olds. This would give parents £1,100 to buy a nursery place where they can find one— private or public. A pilot scheme started in 1996 but many local authorities refused to co-operate with the scheme, arguing that it would undermine their own provision.

Day nurseries and play groups are the responsibility of the social work department. Day nurseries have longer hours than nursery schools and can take children from only a few months to school entry age. These are in the charge of qualified social workers or nursery nurses. Play groups are usually run by groups of individuals who come together to provide some sort of daytime activity for pre-school children and social work departments will often give these groups grants. It must be noted that there is no statutory obligation on a local authority to provide pre-school facilities or services in its area.

Post-school education has been changed radically in the last few years. It may be simpler to divide this into formal and informal education. Previously local authorities were responsible for both areas including advanced further education. Now formal further education, *i.e.* courses leading to some type of qualification, is provided by further education colleges which are independent of the local authorities. Some of these colleges doing degree and similar courses have been made into universities, *e.g.* Glasgow Caledonian University and Napier University.

Local education authorities nevertheless still provide other post-school educational opportunities. This sector is known as community education and embraces the various evening classes in subjects ranging from archaeology to zoology. Community education is mostly paid for from the council's own revenue—it does not attract central government money—and fees. This means that when cutbacks have to be made the unwelcome choice of cutting classes or raising fees has to be made.

Educational authorities also provide what might be described as non-educational services. For instance there are special services such as school health (including school dentists), school meals (including milk), child guidance services, special provision for mentally and physically handicapped children, school transport and school library services.

The private sector of education has always been smaller in Scotland than in the rest of the United Kingdom, amounting to 4 per cent, although the percentage is higher in Edinburgh. Recent legislation has sought to encourage the growth of this area at the expense, some would argue, of the public sector. The Assisted Places Scheme was introduced in 1981 to allow children of "low income" families to gain access to private education. The Self-Governing Schools etc. (Scotland) Act 1989 allows school boards to "opt-out" of the local authority sector and be financed directly by the Scottish Education Department. This does not make them private schools because they do not charge fees and are still financed from the public sector. This policy, so far, has not been a great success in Scotland where there is a long tradition of public education. The Government also tried to encourage a new type of school called a "technology academy" for students over the age of 15 who showed aptitude in the technology fields. These were to be financed by both the public and private sectors. So far only one such school has been set up.

Social Work

Education may be regarded as one of the older local authority services but social work is one of the newer services. Prior to 1969 burgh and county councils shared responsibilities for child welfare and general welfare in the community. The Social Work (Scotland) Act 1968, however, redefined social work. The Act confers on local authorities a general duty to promote social welfare in their areas. This is often seen as

having a responsibility for "vulnerable" groups, *e.g.* children
in need of care, old people and the mentally and physically
handicapped, but the Act is much more general than this,
allowing local authorities a measure of responsibility for
communities which may have special problems. The wording
of the Act is very comprehensive:

> "It shall be the duty of every local authority to promote
> social welfare by making available advice, guidance and
> assistance on such a scale as may be appropriate for
> their area" (s.12(1)).

Given this comprehensiveness it is less easy to describe the
range of work encompassed by the term "social work" than it
is to define the term "education". By the very nature of the
work much will depend on individual and local circumstances. In many ways it would be easier to describe social
work as taking on the problems which are not the direct
responsibility of other local authority services or national
government departments and agencies.

A brief description of social work cannot do justice to the
wide range of activities of a social work department but we
can best see this in terms of groups. Local authority social
work responsibilities include children "at risk", *i.e.* those who
have little or no parental care. Authorities will provide
residential or day facilities for these children either through
group homes or fostering. Although the children's panel or
hearing system is not the responsibility of local authorities,
social work (and education) departments are closely involved
in the work of these panels. As has been previously mentioned, social work departments have responsibilities for day
nurseries, children's homes and residential nurseries,
together with concern for pre-school playgroups. In terms of
family care the work of the department here covers general
support and financial assistance, homes for mothers and
babies, home helps, temporary accommodation and responsibilities for homelessness. This latter responsibility cuts
across local government services since homeless persons are
the responsibility of the social work departments but the
provision of a house is the responsibility of the housing
departments. It was for this reason that the Wheatley Report
had recommended that housing and social work be the
responsibility of one (the regional) authority. This was
rejected by the Conservative Government in 1973 when

housing was given to the districts. It is ironical that the new authorities will be going back to the Wheatley principles.

The mentally and physically disabled are also looked after by the social work departments who invariably try to keep a register of these groups of people and provide homes, care, day centres, training and employment. This type of care often overlaps with care for the elderly. In this respect "meals on wheels" and "lunch clubs" are a regular feature of many community centres. Other types of care for the elderly include home helps, day centres, clubs and homes. It may be added here that where a local authority has a concessionary fare system for local transport, the subsidy to the transport undertaking is paid for from the social work budget.

Amongst what might be regarded as miscellaneous social work provision is the supervision and after-care of adults on probation, together with social work in prisons and young offenders' institutions. More recently social work departments have been involved in safe neighbourhood schemes and projects supporting victims of alcohol and drug abuse and people with AIDS. Social workers are increasingly involved in the work of the National Health Service and co-operate with a wide range of voluntary and charity organisations.

Government policy for health and social work during the 1990s shifted the accent from institutional care to care in the community. This inevitably created more responsibilities for social work departments. Increased co-operation had to develop between social work and the National Health Service. This has led to Planning Agreements between social work departments and the local health boards (and trusts). These agreements have to outline common goals, funding arrangements including provision for joint funding and policy on operational areas. This is intended to eliminate overlapping and duplication although it must be remembered that health boards are concerned with the medical and clinical aspects of their clients while the social work departments are only concerned with their responsibilities under the Social Work Act 1968.

The Social Work Services Group of the Scottish Home and Health Department is responsible for the supervision and oversight of social work services in Scotland, including the funding of voluntary organisations. Since 1992 there has existed a Chief Inspector of Social Work Services who is responsible for inspecting and evaluating the quality of social work provided by local authorities and the other agencies involved. The Social Work Services Group has also been responsible for creating adequate training for social workers in Scotland and provides money to local authorities specifically for this purpose.

Housing

The responsibilities of housing authorities fall into three categories—assessment of needs, building operations and management. Currently housing authorities have to submit to the Secretary of State for Scotland housing plans, which basically are forward plans as to how the local authorities see the housing needs in their areas being met. This means that housing authorities have overall responsibility for housing policy in their area and are not just concerned, as many think, with council houses.

Assessment of need is a very wide responsibility for housing authorities since it requires gathering information about how people are housed and what demand there might be for all types of public and private housing in their area. Such an exercise also requires local authorities to assess housing conditions. In this respect the central government lays down a minimum acceptable standard—the tolerable standard. Housing authorities will then have to decide what to do with houses which are "below the tolerable standard". To demolish requires that the inhabitants have to be rehoused and the ability of a local authority to do this is determined by the availability of houses in the area.

If there is a shortfall between supply and demand the local authority will have to decide how this can be made up. Leaving aside the private housebuilding sector over which the local authority has little control, except perhaps by making land available and designating residential land through the structure and local plan system, the authority has two options—build new houses or improve existing houses.

The building of new houses by a local authority has been severely restricted in recent years as a consequence of Conservative Government policy. The Government's view has been based on three principles: first, that council house rents in Scotland have been too low; secondly, that tenants should be encouraged to buy their council houses; and thirdly, that the private rented sector should be encouraged.

Housing finance will be dealt with in Chapter 5 but it should be pointed out here that housing accounts are required to be kept separate from the accounts of the rest of the authority's services (general services). Successive governments have tried to force local authorities to balance their housing accounts without resorting to subsidies from the revenue acounts. In other words, council housing should be self-financing. Central government has continually limited these subsidies to the housing account and the capital allocation became restricted or disappeared altogether. The consequences of these events was that many local authorities had no money to build new council houses or provide adequate maintenance or management services.

The Government's policy of encouraging council house sales has also had its consequences on house building. By giving considerable discounts (sometimes up to 70 per cent) to sitting tenants to buy their houses, this reduced the stock of "good" houses, *i.e.* those requiring less maintenance costs and those in the more desirable areas. However, local authorities had borrowed money on the 100 per cent cost when building the houses and still had to pay back the original loan. Further, the housing stock which remained was generally of the older type and required more maintenance. Councils, therefore, found it difficult to raise capital for new houses.

With the difficulties of building new houses, central government has been encouraging local authorities to move in two other directions, either to help improve older houses or enter into "joint venture" housing with the private building sector.

Nowadays local authorities have three methods of improving older houses—grants and loans to owners, improvement of the housing authorities' own houses or the buying up of old houses and handing over these to housing associations. All of this is often described as rehabilitation. Housing associations are groups of owners or tenants in an area who receive grants from Scottish Homes to improve their property on a collective basis. This mainly applies to tenement property.

With little or no capital for council house building, many councils were forced to come to some sort of arrangement with the private sector if houses were to be built at all. Since local authorities own a considerable amount of land, the solution was an arrangement where the council supplied the land and the builder built the houses either for sale or for cost rent. In either case the houses are outside the council's ownership and control.

One other method of providing houses should be mentioned here. Central government has been trying to persuade local authorities to hand over houses directly to Scottish Homes which then, in turn, funds tenant co-operatives or housing associations. Although the local authority may retain some nomination rights for a certain number of its tenants, the houses are no longer owned by the authority.

The third responsibility of housing authorities is the maintenance and management of its own stock of houses. Local authorities are usually the largest landlords in an area and, as such, have the normal duties and responsibilities of a landlord, *i.e.* to keep their property in good repair. Due to the restrictions put on subsidies to the housing account many local authorities have found it difficult to meet their obligation to maintain property, resulting in "void" houses, *i.e.* houses without tenants. If the authority cannot repair these houses they remain empty for long periods with a consequent loss of rents, thus exacerbating the problem. In addition to this, housing authorities have a responsibility in the area of estate management—trying to keep the environment (fences, grassed areas, etc.) in good order. As landlords, housing authorities are also concerned with rent collection, with transferring tenants from house to house if the tenants wish to transfer and, more recently, with the administration of the central government's housing benefit scheme. It is in this last area that there is another overlap with the social work services.

As mentioned earlier, housing authorities are not just concerned with their own houses. Under a variety of housing and public health legislation local authorities can control conditions for private tenants, particularly in multi-occupancy houses. Local authorities have the power to take over a house from a landlord under this legislation.

The Housing (Scotland) Act 1988 gives tenants the right, in addition to their right to buy, to choose a landlord other than the local authority so long as that landlord is registered with Scottish Homes as a suitable landlord. The New Town corporations in Scotland are being wound up and the tenants of these corporations are being offered a choice of landlords, including the local housing associations and the new unitary authorities in their area.

This development has to be seen alongside other provisions of the same Act which created Scottish Homes, a public agency, to take on the responsibilities of the former Housing

Corporation and the Scottish Special Housing Association. This agency can become a landlord, not for individual tenants, but for groups of tenants in part or all of a council housing estate who might want to opt for Scottish Homes as their landlord. The Government however has been encouraging Scottish Homes to hand over such houses to recognised housing associations. The eventual aim is that Scottish Homes will not be concerned directly in the management of public housing but will simply be a builder and co-ordinator of housing association houses.

It can be seen from the above details that there has been a profound change during the last few years in council housing which has considerably reduced the responsibilities of local authorities although they still retain a strategic role with regard to housing in their area. Not surprisingly local authorities have seen these developments as another example of the reduction of their powers.

Planning

Under the 1973 Act planning was a "concurrent function". Strategic planning, including the preparation and updating of a structure plan, was the responsibility of regional and island authorities. Local planning was the responsibility of district councils. Under the 1994 Act local authorities are required to form joint committees to carry out their functions in connection with structure planning. The Secretary of State has designated the structure plan areas.

Strategic planning includes research and intelligence, strategic economic planning, land use planning, industrial and urban development and the countryside. Under the 1973 Act and various Town and Country Planning Acts the regional (and islands) authorities had the responsibility to produce a "structure plan". This plan was based on population trends and was concerned not only with the size of the population but its location. The aim of the structure plan was to try to set objectives for all the local government services in each region and as such was concerned with what economists would call "resource allocation". By its very nature, therefore, strategic planning is about infrastructure.

Both the Wheatley Report and the 1973 Act recognised that some district authorities would be too small to deal with even local planning. For this reason local planning, development control, building control, listed buildings and conservation areas were the responsibility of the regional authorities in the Highlands, Borders and Dumfries and Galloway. However, in these areas the regions devised an organisation whereby the district authorities (members and officials) were involved in local planning decisions by means of a type of liaison committee. The 1994 Act seems to suggest that this system should be continued albeit under the idea of "decentralisation" which will be described later.

Local planning includes local land use and development control. Legislation requires planning authorities to prepare local plans, each of which has to fit into the broad approach of the structure plan. There are three types of local plans. District plans cover all or part of a former district authority's area. The broad strategy has been laid out in the structure plan and the details for implementation are set out in the local plan. In the smaller districts there may have been only one plan for the area whereas larger districts may have been broken up into a number of areas. Action area plans are usually designated in the structure plan and are areas requiring improvement or redevelopment. Subject plans are those which explain policy on a particular subject such as commercial development, industrial estates or tourist facilities.

Development control is concerned, amongst other things, with the change of use of land and buildings, and encompasses anything from house extensions to major town centre development and advertisements to tree preservation. It is not necessary to go into a detailed description of the procedure for planning applications. Broadly speaking developers will submit their application to the planning authority. There are statutory requirements to inform interested parties such as neighbours. Council officials will usually discuss problems with the developer and explain council policy, *e.g.* style of windows, limits on the height of buildings, and what is acceptable in a conservation area. In the larger type of development, particularly near a local government boundary, there may also have to be discussions with a neighbouring local authority about, for instance, impact on transportation, parking or road safety.

The planning committee will then discuss the proposal. Before this stage is reached it is likely that councillors will have been "lobbied" by both supporters of and objectors to the proposal. The committee has delegated powers to make final decisions. The committee can make one of three decisions. Permission may be granted, refused or granted subject to conditions. In the case of refusal the reasons must be on planning grounds based in the Planning Acts and not on political (or whimsical) grounds. If an application is refused or granted conditionally the developer has the right to appeal to the Secretary of State for Scotland.

The Secretary of State may set up a public inquiry and/or approve or refuse the application. Whatever decision the Secretary of State makes overrides the planning authority's decision and there is no appeal except to the courts on a point of law. The Secretary of State also has powers to "call in" any planning application if he thinks the development would affect central government policy or where there might be conflict between two authorities. Before 1996 regional authorities were able to arbitrate conflicts of interest between the district councils in their area and to "call in" applications. It is to be presumed that the absence of regional arbitration will give more power to the Secretary of State.

The post-war Planning Acts designated areas around cities as "green belts" where it was expected that no further developments should take place. This was to provide a "lung" for city dwellers within easy reach of a city centre. Throughout the post-war years, however, local authorities have come under considerable pressure to release land in the green belt mainly for housing development. It is argued that releasing some of this land reduces land (and therefore house) prices. The counter-argument is that allowing encroachments on the green belt will increase urbanisation and reduce leisure activities. Conservative Secretaries of State have tended to allow certain encroachments on the green belt if they have felt this would reduce house prices but have balanced this with certain conditions about the number of houses per hectare. However, overall it would appear that reductions of the green belt have been compensated for by taking in land previously undesignated, thus keeping a rough balance.

Transportation

At the time of the 1975 reorganisation of local government the new regional and islands authorities were responsible for a range of transport facilities including trunk roads (and bridges), traffic management, street lighting, street parking and (in the cities) bus services. All of this required considerable expenditure of both capital and revenue. Most transport authorities were able to use funds from the European Community to build roads where these were associated with industrial development or urban renewal.

However, since 1975 local authorities in the cities have lost their bus services. In 1985 city bus services were "deregulated". This meant that the running of city bus services was handed over to private companies albeit that all the shares in those companies were owned by the respective regional councils. Since then the Government has encouraged the buyout of these companies by employees and managers. Deregulation also meant that other private companies could bid to the regional authorities for certain or all of the routes in the city. For a time this led to some confusion but there has been a rationalisation of services. It seems likely that a further process of rationalisation and privatisation will develop in the rural and urban transport systems.

One consequence of the creation of unitary authorities is that subsidies which were given by regional authorities to bus services and also to British Rail to provide region-wide services may now be ended or at least fragmented. An instance of possible fragmentation is the Strathclyde Passenger Transport Authority ("SPTA"). SPTA, over the years, developed a region-wide rail system in conjunction with British Rail. However, with the new system of local government it seems unlikely that, say, Glasgow Council will wish to continue subsidies for services outside Glasgow. SPTA will have representatives of each of the councils in the area but may find its finances restricted by council "infighting".

As far as road building and maintenence is concerned the idea of regional planning of a road network will end. In this respect, under the 1994 Act, the Secretary of State for Scotland has taken increased powers in order to ensure a consistency of road building and co-ordination between the new transportation authorities. At the end of this reorganisation the new authorities are left with very localised powers dealing with lighting, parking and traffic management, all of which are closely regulated and supervised by the Scottish Office.

Environmental Services

The responsibilities in this category of services are diverse but are mainly concerned with creating a good environment and some of the services here are fundamental to urban living. The functions included are cleansing and refuse collection; baths and washhouses; regulation of shops, offices, markets and slaughterhouses; food hygiene; and burial and cremation. In the past these were often described as public health.

Cleansing and refuse disposal include street cleaning and refuse collection and disposal. Although all these aspects are important it is refuse disposal which is a big expenditure item to local authorities. The extent of modern packaging is such that more equipment is required to cope with this. However, recent years have seen an increased interest in recycling of waste or packaging materials and local authorities are only too conscious of their responsibilities in this area. It is an option to reduce costs of collection by separation of different types of waste material—bottles, waste paper, metal, etc. and many authorities have invested heavily in this.

Local authorities have considerable statutory powers and responsibilities in respect of the regulation of public premises and standards of food hygiene. Here the local authority will inspect premises regularly and also investigate complaints from members of the public. This type of service is done unobtrusively but it is often taken for granted by the public who would soon complain if standards were to be lowered or if there was not adequate inspection, particularly of food shops, restaurants, public houses, etc.

Environmental health authorities also have responsibilities for various types of pollution—air, noise and, more recently, radiation. Since the Chernobyl accident authorities have been monitoring nuclear establishments for possible leakages and pollution of land, water and air.

The Scottish Environmental Protection Agency has taken over some local authority functions in respect of environmental services: see page 33 below.

Recreation

The reorganisation of 1975 gave local authorities the opportunity to amalgamate a wide range of activities under this heading. They are normally described as "recreation" or "recreation and leisure" and are often divided into physical recreation and cultural recreation. There is provision of parks, sports centres, swimming pools, libraries, museums, art galleries and often municipal theatres.

However the scale of these activities and past tradition has often meant that the former district authorities did not carry out all the above services. From 1975 to 1982 recreation, particularly physical recreation, was a "concurrent" function which meant that both regions and districts could make provision. Some regions took the opportunity to do this, especially where there were party political differences between region and district as in Lothian and Edinburgh. After the Stodart Committee recommendations in 1982 were enacted the districts became the providers of these services. The 1994 Act will resolve any differences of management that may have existed from previous years.

In the Highlands, Borders and Dumfries and Galloway regions it was found impossible, under the 1973 Act, to separate libraries from the education service, and consequently this was a regional function. It is obvious that the services for cultural recreation are even more connected to education. As with physical recreation it is schoolchildren and students who will be the main consumers. The 1994 Act should help to improve co-ordination between recreation and education.

In a later section we shall consider the growth of compulsory competitive tendering but at this point it may be said that some aspects of physical recreation have been privatised, for instance, facilities like bowling greens, tennis courts and golf courses.

Miscellaneous

The above description of services covers the major responsibilities of the new unitary authorities. However there are a number of other functions for which local authorities are responsible, many of them previously exercised by the district councils. Only a brief description will be given here.

Closely associated with the planning process is building control. This function, particularly in the cities, is a successor to the old Dean of Guild Courts which were abolished in 1975. Building control deals with both new buildings and alterations to existing buildings either externally or internally. Applications are scrutinised to make sure that the plans conform to the various (national) building codes. Building control is also concerned with public safety. Thus any building which, for one reason or another, appears to threaten public safety will be inspected and appropriate action taken. This includes fire and safety regulations regarding public buildings and also the structural state of all buildings. Building control officials monitor the structural state of all buildings in their area particularly older buildings. Should any building appear to be unsafe building control officials will secure it and may even recommend demolition. Anyone altering a building without building control permission may be requested to restore the building to its original condition. Building control committees act, similar to planning committees, in a non-political and quasi-judicial capacity.

The administration of district courts has been passed to the new authorities, although the actual court infrastructure has remained in place. District courts deal with offences ranging from parking and traffic offences to theft, breach of the peace and assault, where the maximum fine is £2,500 or 60 days in jail. Since 1996, district courts have been responsible for a further range of fixed penalties including certain drug offences. The justices in the district courts are appointed by the Secretary of State on the advice of J.P. advisory committees. The local authority also nominates up to a quarter of its members to serve as *ex officio* members. Only in Glasgow are there full-time professional justices called stipendiary magistrates.

Local authorities have considerable powers of licensing. This is usually exercised by two committees. Public house and liquor licensing is the responsibility of licensing boards made up of councillors but not subject to the overall control of the full council. Other licensing may be the responsibility of a licensing or general purposes committee which acts in a quasi-judicial capacity, *i.e.* its decisions are rarely taken to the full council. The range of licensing here is extensive including public entertainment, street trading, markets, taxis and specialist trading like second-hand dealers and pawnbrokers.

Since 1982 two other functions, which had been concurrent functions under the 1973 Act, became more the responsibility of district councils. Economic development by local authorities has increased due to a number of factors. Many local authorities realised that often they had land available for development and had power, under the planning laws, to determine the use of land. Joint ventures with the private sector were therefore developed leading to retail and industrial estates. Secondly, because of compulsory competitive tendering (to be described later), local authorities could set up businesses of their own. Thirdly, these developments were made easier because of the Conservative Government's commitment to private enterprise and deregulation.

Throughout Scotland tourism has become a major industry and local authorities are closely involved in this. Before 1982 this also had been a concurrent function but one of the results of giving it solely to the district councils was that some of these councils were too small to exercise this function adequately. The Government, therefore, created area tourist boards which largely replaced the local authority tourist activities albeit that the councils were represented on the boards. These ATBs were, effectively, the regional organisations of the Scottish Tourist Board. The 1994 Act empowers the Secretary of State for Scotland to establish new area tourist boards which came into operation in April 1996. Local authorities will be represented on these boards and can give financial assistance to them. The Act also empowers local authorities to discharge some of their tourist-related activities to the boards. Some local authorities, particularly in the cities, have been resentful of these ATBs, feeling that they understand their area better than any other organisation but also resentful of the loss of total control.

The above description of the many functions of local authorities disguises a subtle change in the exercise of these functions. Many of these functions could be described as local monopolies. The Conservative Government's philosophy has been that monopolies, national or local, are inefficient. It feels that local government services should be subject to competition. The first example of this approach was the deregulation of municipal bus services in 1985. The Local Government Act 1988 took this approach further.

The main provisions of this Act defined the notion of compulsory competitive tendering (CCT) in certain local government services. The Act listed a number of activities which were to be exposed to competition. These "defined activities" included: building cleaning; street cleaning; school and welfare catering; other catering; maintenance of ground; and repair and maintenance of vehicles. The Act allows the Secretary of State to add further activities to the list and, so far, sport and leisure management, street repairs and council house maintenance have been added. There is a current proposal to include legal and administrative services in the "defined activities". The response of local authorities to this legislation was to set up, within the council administration, Direct Service Organisations (DSOs) and Direct Labour Organisations (DLOs) to enable council employees ("in house") to tender for these services in competition with outside contractors. These DSOs and DLOs are autonomous and self-financing organisations within the council. However one area of contention between local authorities and the Government has been the extent of "overheads"—the cost of administering these organisations is often borne by the local authority and the Government argues that this gives the DSOs and DLOs an unfair advantage, hence the proposal to open up legal and administrative services to competition. So far local authority DSOs and DLOs have been largely successful in winning tenders, probably because the personnel "in place" have had more knowledge of the working of the system than outside contractors. Under the reorganised system there have been a number of problems because some region-wide DSOs and DLOs, many of which won contracts, will have to be broken up unless the new councils in the area can come to some arrangement to continue them.

The above descriptions are of local government functions but, as previously mentioned, local authorities have lost some functions and the 1994 Act continued the trend away from direct council control of some services. The undernoted functions are now generally exercised by joint boards established by the Secretary of State under the 1994 Act—a system prevalent in the 1929 local government system but much reduced in the system established by the 1975 Act.

Valuation

In order to levy both council and business taxes there has to be valuation of property. Under the 1973 Act this was mainly in the hands of the regional authorities with special arrangements for the Highlands and Islands. Under the 1994 Act each local authority area shall be a valuation area but with joint boards to oversee the work of the assessor and his/her staff. Each chief assessor, although appointed by the board, is independent of control from the councils represented on the board.

Police

It was always difficult to include the police as a wholly local government service. Under the 1973 Act the police were organised roughly in accordance with regional boundaries except that Lothian and Borders had one police force and the Northern Constabulary covered the Highland Region, Orkney, Shetland and the Western Isles. Under the 1994 Act the eight police authorities are retained (along with their names) although they are overseen by joint boards representing the respective unitary authorities. The only exceptions to this are in Fife and Dumfries and Galloway where the new authority is the same as the previous regional council. Police authorities appoint chief constables subject to the approval of the Secretary of State but these authorities have no control over operational matters, *i.e.* uniformed branch, criminal investigation and traffic wardens. The joint boards only have some say in equipping the police force and ensuring its proper administration. Despite the minimum control of the police force, police authorities contribute 49 per cent of expenditure, the other 51 per cent coming directly from the Scottish Office.

Fire

Unlike the police the fire service is much more a local government service. Here the fire authority has power to vary the establishment, appoint officers, control equipment and buildings and concern itself with operational matters. The service is, however, managed by joint boards representing the respective local authorities. The areas of these joint boards are similar to that of the police except that, under the 1994 Act, Strathclyde Fire Service has become the Mid and South Western fire service and Lothian and Borders Fire Service has become the South Eastern fire service. It is difficult to understand the thinking behind this change of name.

Water and Sewerage

One of the biggest, and most controversial, changes in the 1994 Act applies to water and sewerage. This service was, until 1996, the responsibility of regional authorities. However, reorganisation took this service out of the direct control of the new local authorities. From 1996 there have been three boards—West, East and North—whose members have been appointed by the Secretary of State. These charge a water rate and a separate sewerage rate which are paid directly to the water and sewerage authorities except that local authorities can collect the charges for dwellings. The controversy arises because the Government has privatised water and sewerage in England and Wales and the suspicion is that by taking this service out of the direct control of local government and setting up three large authorities the Government is preparing the ground for privatisation. There is little doubt that this would be very unpopular in Scotland if a referendum in Strathclyde is any guide—98 per cent of those who voted were against privatisation.

River Purification

River purification boards were set up under the 1973 Act. The representation on these boards was one-third from the regions, one-third from the districts and one-third appointed by the Secretary of State for Scotland to represent the various interests in the board's area. The 1994 Act retained the boards but changed the representation. This temporary arrangement was superseded by the creation of the Scottish Environmental Protection Agency, effective April 1, 1996, which has taken over all functions formerly exercised by the river purification boards.

Children's Hearings

Although the children's hearings or panel system was not an integrated service of local government the regional authorities had a considerable input both in cash and advice through their social work departments and in the appointment of reporters. The Government took the opportunity of the 1994 Act to centralise the system. From 1996 this service has been called the Scottish Children's Reporter Administration with a Principal Reporter and area reporters. The agency is financed solely by the Scottish Office and the staff of the previous (regional) panels were transferred to the new agency. The Principal Reporter, however, still relies on the reports on children from the council social work departments.

Convention of Scottish Local Authorities

Before 1975 there was no one voice which spoke for the interests of local authorities. There were instead four national organisations which reflected the structure of the old local government system, the oldest of which was the Convention of Royal Burghs. Since 1975 there has been only one organisation—the Convention of Scottish Local Authorities (COSLA).

The main objectives of COSLA are threefold. First, to protect and promote the interests and the rights of member authorities, particularly with regard to proposed legislation. Secondly, to act as a discussion forum for matters of mutual interest to the local authorities. In this respect it acts as a "clearing house" of information by collecting the views of its members and conveying these views to other local authority organisations (in the United Kingdom) or to the government. Thirdly, it is concerned with providing essential services like the National Joint Council (on wages) and training information to the member authorities.

At the time of writing there are no decisions as to the structure of the Convention under the new system of local government. The old Convention was complicated by the existence of three types of authorities but, with unitary authorities, it seems likely that the new structure will be simpler although there may still have to be "weighting" of committee representation in favour of rural authorities who are in the minority *vis-à-vis* the urban authorities. It is likely that the structure will be based on function committees with some other general committees. Although the new Convention may allow over-representation of rural councils the financing will remain the same—each council contributing on the basis of population.

Much of the work of the Convention is concerned with matters arising from legislation and government policy. In this sense it acts as adviser to the government. This is particularly so when it comes to the various grant settlements each year. Another aspect of the Convention's work is to try to get standards laid down so that there is not too much variation in the provision of services between one local authority and another. However, any recommendation from COSLA to member authorities is only advisory and not compulsory.

CHAPTER 3

COUNCILLORS, COMMITTEES AND DEPARTMENTS

As was mentioned in Chapter 1, local government in Scotland has a long history preceding a structured central administration. However until the nineteenth century its personnel could not be described as representative of the local citizens. Even in the nineteenth century councillors were elected by a minority of the citizens. Thus, in a sense, increased powers for local authorities in the twentieth century have matched the increasing size of the electorate. As the electorate increased in numbers so the need to organise election campaigns grew. Although political parties were organised at parliamentary elections they were slow to develop a strategy for local elections. In effect, party politics in local government is a very recent development.

As the powers and responsibilities of local councils grew, it became necessary to organise the business of the council. Unlike the parliamentary system, and perhaps because of the low profile of party politics, local authorities used a committee system and not a cabinet system, with departmental officials responsible to a committee rather than to a minister as in the Westminster model. Despite attempts at reforming that committee system it remains the basic structure of Scottish local government.

Elections

Local government elections have attracted their share of criticism because of low turnout and the intrusion of "national politics". Despite this the procedures used have changed very little. Much of the legislation on qualifications and procedures has survived local government reform and only arrangements for boundary changes have altered with the creation of the Local Government Boundary Commission.

Voting qualifications for local elections do not significantly differ from qualifications for parliamentary elections. Those entitled to be registered and to vote must be:

(a) resident in the local authority area on the qualifying date (usually October 10 each year);

(b) not subject to any legal incapacity to vote, and either a British subject or a citizen of the Republic of Ireland; and

(c) of voting age on the date of the poll, *i.e.* 18 years or over.

Those who are not 18 by the date the register is published (February 15) but who will reach that age during the currency of the register have the date of their birthday against their name and can vote at any election taking place on or after their birthday. Commonwealth citizens are entitled to be registered and to vote, as are European citizens (since January 1, 1996).

Certain categories of electors are entitled to vote by post or proxy. Electors who are unable to vote in person (absent voters) because of their occupation or employment or because of blindness or other physical incapacity, or because they would have to make a journey by sea or air from their qualifying address to the polling station, can apply to vote by post or proxy. Since 1985 the rules for postal or proxy voting have been extended and the returning officer has more discretion about who qualifies for postal or proxy votes. It is also possible for a proxy voter to vote, on the elector's behalf, by post. Applications for a postal or proxy vote must be received by the last day for nominations.

Election procedure is fairly well established in Scottish local government and is contained in the Representation of the People Act 1983, as amended 1985, and supplemented by various statutory instruments issued from time to time. Under the 1994 Act the first ordinary elections for the new unitary councils were held on April 6, 1995 except in Orkney, Shetland and the Western Isles which had had elections in 1994 and were not subject to much change in the reform process. The second ordinary elections for all councils will be held in 1999 with subsequent elections every three years. Unlike the 1973 Act, which set the elections on the first Thursday in May, the 1994 Act provides for elections either on that date or on such other date as the Secretary of State for

Scotland may fix, subject to adequate (15 months') notice. It can be assumed that these elections will normally be held in May.

Candidate nominations require two proposers and eight others. Together with the name of the candidate a "description not exceeding six words" is allowed. This permits candidates to put the name of the political party which they are representing. Candidates normally appoint an election agent although they can act as their own agent. It is the agent's responsibility to deal with the legal and financial arrangements for the election and it is the agent who is held responsible if election law is breached. In addition to these procedural responsibilities the election agent will organise most aspects of the candidate's campaign including the raising of sufficient money.

The cost of an election campaign is limited by law. For local government elections this limit is set at a flat rate plus so many pence per entry on the electoral register in each ward. The amount is reviewed and updated before elections. Candidates, however, are allowed free use of schools for public meetings though they are not allowed free distribution to election addresses as in parliamentary elections. There are certain requirements laid down about the campaign, *e.g.* committee rooms cannot be in polling stations; all literature must have the name of an election agent; no canvassing or loudspeakers are allowed outside polling stations.

On election day the hours of polling are 8.00 a.m. to 9.00 p.m. and are now the same for all local authorities. There is no provision for an extension of hours. In addition to an election agent each candidate is allowed to appoint polling agents. The number of polling agents is usually laid down by the returning officer. Polling agents act as the candidate's agent at the polling stations. Only candidates, their election agent and polling agents are allowed to attend polling stations to check for personation, etc.

Procedure at the counting of ballot papers is uniform. The ballot boxes are first sealed and then conveyed to the central counting station. At the central counting station the total votes cast are counted first and checked against the counterfoils. This is to ensure that no ballot papers have been lost (or added!). Each candidate's votes are then counted (usually in bundles of 100) and doubtful ballot papers, *e.g.* the "X" overlapping two names, are adjudicated by candidates and the presiding officer. Each candidate is allowed a prescribed

number of counting agents—the number is laid down by the
returning officer—who ensure that the proper procedure is
carried out by the counting clerks. Ballot papers and "marked
registers" (which give a record of those who have voted
although not how they voted) are kept for six months and
then destroyed.

Councillors

Councillors have also come in for criticism in recent years
with claims that they have become too "professional" and
"political". Nevertheless there are still standard requirements
which councillors have to adhere to and these, as in the
elections, have changed little over the years.

There are certain qualifications necessary to be elected as a
councillor. A candidate must be 21 years old or more (note
that the voting age is 18 years); be a British subject or citizen
of the Irish Republic; be a local government elector within the
area of the local authority or have resided or have their
principal place of work in the area of the authority for 12
months preceding their nomination.

There are also a number of factors which disqualify a
person from standing for election in local government.
Persons who hold a paid office at the disposal of the local
authority or of a joint committee to which the authority is
party are disqualified, as are persons who are undischarged
bankrupts or who have been disqualified for corrupt or illegal
practices.

Once in office councillors have certain legal obligations. If a
member of a local authority fails, through a period of six
consecutive months, to attend any meeting of the authority he
shall, unless the authority has approved of such absence,
cease to be a councillor. Vacancies, by death or resignation,
are filled by a by-election except if such vacancy occurs
within six months of the next ordinary election of the council.
A person filling a casual vacancy holds office only until the
next ordinary election.

Other legal obligations pertain to financial interest and
surcharge. Numerous Acts and regulations set out procedures for financial interest. The main provisions are in
regard to pecuniary and non-pecuniary interests. With regard
to pecuniary interests the member must declare an interest
and refrain from taking part in the discussion and any vote
on the matter. Breach of these requirements is a criminal

offence. Non-pecuniary interests are less easy to define but include such things as being related to someone tendering for a contract or applying for a council job. It is not a criminal offence if no declaration is made but most councillors will declare to be on the safe side. Since 1989 councillors are obliged to register direct and indirect pecuniary interests or no interest at all.

If a member of a local authority authorises the misapplication or improper spending of the authority's funds he or she can be surcharged and ordered to reimburse the amount misspent. Although such cases are rare there have been examples, particulary over the poll tax campaign, which have served to point to the tension between central and local government.

Allegations of mis-spending are referred to the Commission for Local Authority Accounts in Scotland—now known as the Accounts Commission for Scotland. If the Controller of Audit, who is the chief officer of the Commission, after investigating the allegation, believes that there has been mis-spending he brings this to the attention of the Commission and the local authority concerned. The Commission, who are lay members appointed by the Secretary of State for Scotland, may bring the Secretary of State's attention to the matter. It is then for the Secretary of State to decide what action, if any, should be taken. It is possible for the councillors concerned to challenge the Controller's view in court but such action, in itself, could be construed as misuse of public money.

The Local Government and Housing Act 1989 changed the system of councillors' remuneration. The 1973 Act had introduced attendance allowances, while the Local Government and Planning (Scotland) Act 1982 added the choice, for councillors, to claim either attendance allowance or financial loss allowance. The 1989 Act, while retaining the attendance and financial loss systems, altered the remuneration system in two ways. First, it set a limit on the maximum claimable amount in an attempt to "cap" councillors' allowances. Because this inhibited and restricted senior councillors' posts (like chairpersons) the Act, secondly, introduced the idea of a special responsibility allowance for these positions. Most councils pay a flat rate (currently £5,000 to £6,000) plus special responsibility allowances determined by each council. Financial loss allowance was abolished in 1991 and since 1995 there has been no maximum limit on the special responsibility allowance.

Political Parties

There has always been an ambiguous attitude to the role of political parties in the British political system. On the one hand they have been seen as important in mobilising the vote while, on the other hand, they have not, until recently, been recognised in law. Even the Representation of the People Act 1983 does not bend to the recognition of parties but allows candidates to put "a description", not exceeding six words, after their names on the ballot paper.

Political parties in local government have been even less accepted. The tradition that an elected representative serves the public and not a particular sector of the public is even stronger in local government than in national politics. There had been controversy over full-time paid councillors and this underlined the idea of voluntary public service. However, as in national politics, with the growth of the franchise and the growth of an ideological base to politics, party machines have developed since the middle of the nineteenth century. The Labour Party, although late on the scene in national politics, was first on the scene in local politics with its ideas of "municipal socialism" in the 1890s. From then the Labour Party's attitudes to the role of the party in local government fluctuated, depending on its success at the national level. Only after 1945 did the Labour Party become involved extensively in local government, resulting in the Conservative Party, with much reluctance, entering the local government arena.

In Scotland, the Labour Party intervened in local government in the urban areas (including large towns) and only very exceptionally in rural areas. This is still very much the case. The Conservatives (or Unionists as they often described themselves) in Scotland were even more reluctant than their English colleagues to enter the fray in local elections, leaving their interests to be promoted by local "Progressives" or "Independents". However, as in 1945, with the return of a Labour government in 1964 the Conservatives in Scotland decided at their conference in 1965 to contest local elections in those areas where the Labour Party was in control.

Since local government reorganisation in 1974–75 political parties have been more in evidence. The reasons for this are quite simple. The regional authorities had more power and more resources at their disposal. Control of the regional authority was therefore seen, not as an extension of the local party's power, but an adjunct to the national party's effort to control central government.

The Scottish political scene has also changed with fluctuating support for the Scottish National Party and the appearance on the electoral scene of the Liberal Democratic Party. In addition, what was previously the Ecology Party has now become the Green Party. All of these parties, in addition to the traditional Labour and Conservative parties, enter candidates in local elections as a base for subsequent involvement in national politics.

These developments have helped to reinforce political parties in local elections, particularly in the city and large town areas. Thus, despite the misgivings of many people, the fact has to be recognised that political parties have played, and will continue to play, an important role in local government.

The Council

Many commentators regard the council as a talking-shop or rubber stamp with little power or influence which has been ruined by the injection of party politics into its deliberations. However, the Wheatley Commission did not share this opinion:

> "We believe . . . that the council should be supreme in the direction and control of the affairs of the authority" (para. 946).

Wheatley went on to distinguish three elements in the supremacy of the council. First, the council is, collectively, the body corporate or legal person—property is vested in the council, staff are appointed by the council, charges are levied by the council and powers delegated to committees are exercised in the name of the council. Secondly, major decisions are taken by the council—the broad policies are set, expenditure approved and the budget debated. Thirdly, the council is a forum for public debate and the challenging and questioning of policy and administration:

> "It is in the council chamber that local democracy should be at its most visible" (para. 948).

Council meetings all vary considerably from authority to authority, but within an authority they can also vary. They may be short, uninteresting and uncontroversial but on the other hand they can be long, heated and controversial. Much will depend on factors like political composition, the issues and the interest generated by the public, press or groups.

Let us take two aspects of the full council—those present and the nature of the business transacted. The largest group of those present will be the councillors themselves presided over by the chairman, convener or (lord/lady) provost. Seating patterns vary from council to council and very often depend on party allegiance. Some councils have the continental semi-circular pattern, while others have the parliamentary pattern where the leaders of the two main parties face each other and there are cross-benches for other parties or independents.

The second group of people will be the officials of the council—the chief executive, director of administration, director of finance, committee clerks and other chief officials who may have an interest in the business before the council. The last group of people will be the press and public who are there as observers and take no part in proceedings, unless some deputation from the public is asked to make representations on some topic on the agenda.

One point about the council in relation to the committee system should be mentioned. The method by which any committee reaches a decision is determined by the standing orders of the council and the remit of the particular committee. These are laid down by the council and can only be amended or suspended by the council. Thus, as was said at the beginning of this section, the council is supreme in the decision-making process and, although a committee may take a unanimous decision on an issue, it is still open to the council to overturn that decision, unless it is a decision taken by a committee which has had the power to take the decision delegated to it.

Not all councils are organised along party lines but it may be as well to consider this aspect of council pattern since many are highly political in the party sense of the word. In Scotland, as in England, where parties have representation on a council they are usually organised into party groups on the parliamentary model. This means that those groups will normally meet before a full council meeting and discuss the council agenda, and members are required to abide by the decisions of the group on pain of suspension or expulsion from the group. This is the "party whip" system and it very often applies to committee meetings as well as full council meetings. Councils with a highly developed party system will often give *de facto* recognition to the system—group rooms, secretarial help, regular meetings between group officials and chief officers, etc. Although party organisation may be regretted by some, it may well help to oil the wheels of decision-making although, of course, it will make extra demands on a member's time.

Another aspect of the council is the municipal year and meeting cycle. The first is determined by two events—the election in an election year and the annual budget. Since elections are in April/May, a reconstruction of the leaders of the council and the composition of the committees takes place then. Some councils reconstitute chairman and committee composition each year or every two years irrespective of elections.

The annual budget, however, does not take account of elections. There are specific dates laid down by statute for the submission of budgets by authorities to the Secretary of State for Scotland and these necessarily determine the budget timetable. The local authority financial year has now been brought into line with the central government's financial year. By statute local authorities have to fix their council tax by March each year, which means that the decision on the charges to be levied has usually to be made in the preceding January or February. Committees therefore spend much of their time from December to February reviewing the estimates.

The final aspect of council and committee work to be considered is what might be called information flow. This is the manner by which council or committee decisions are communicated to the public and press. Not long after the Widdicombe Committee's interim report in 1985 the Local Government (Access to Information) Act 1985 was enacted to ensure that the public had a right to more information about the workings of their local authorities and more access to their deliberations. Under this Act members of the public and press have a right to attend committee and sub-committee meetings unless a resolution is passed to discuss an item or a series of items in private—normally described as the "B" agenda. Usually the items discussed in private relate to contracts or personal cases.

As to the publication of minutes, again there is a requirement in the 1973 and 1985 Acts to allow public inspection of council and committee minutes and documents. However, some local authorities, before the 1985 Act, already made these documents available in local libraries, council offices, etc. as a matter of practice.

Taking these two elements together it can be seen that, although a council or committee (or sub-committee) may exclude the press and the public from some (or all) of its proceedings, the minutes of the "private" session can be made available immediately to the public. It is usually the discussion that is confidential and not the decision, and a distinction must be made between the two.

The Committee System

Before the 1975 reform of local government there had been some criticism of the committee system. The system at that time was regarded as inefficient and time-consuming with too much time spent on detail and too little time on long-term planning and policy decisions.

Although proposals for the reform of the committee system were suggested as necessary at the time of the 1975 reorganisation, in this aspect of local government, as with other aspects, the old conventions have been difficult to change, and therefore it is important to be aware of the traditional committee system.

Local authorities have for a long time had the powers to create committees to discharge their functions. Even the smallest local authorities created committees, albeit that every member of council was on every committee. The large authorities created an often very elaborate system of committees.

The committee system has been underwritten by central government departments through the legislative process by insisting that certain local authority functions were exercised through a specific committee, *e.g.* education, social work, planning. Alterations to this system will be discussed later. Since 1973 legislation has allowed a more flexible approach in terms of committees and local authorities have been free to create whichever committees they think necessary.

It is a feature of the committee system that committees spawn sub-committees and sometimes sub-sub-committees. Their size, number and composition are usually determined by the parent committee and they may be temporary or permanent. Sub-committees are frequently used to consider in more detail certain aspects, functions or areas of a council's responsibilities, and since they often wish to consider confidential items, *e.g.* contracts, personal cases, etc., some, or all, of their meetings will be closed to the public. However sub-committees are useful for finding out detailed information from officials about problems or proposals before councillors, or party groups, develop a policy.

The traditional principles underlying the committee system have determined the internal organisation and structure of local authorities. First, services and functions should be clearly identifiable and usually associated with a particular profession, *e.g.* finance, education, social work, roads, *etc.* Secondly, for each service there should be a committee to run it, a chief officer and departmental officials to administer the service. Thus, in summary, we had this form:

one function—one committee—one chief officer—one department.

This was followed through with a part of a service:

one part of a service—one sub-committee—one section head—one section.

This identification of a committee with a service and a department fitted into the attitude of mind that *policy* and *administration* were quite distinct. Thus the committee made the policy and the department implemented it.

Committees and Departments

Probably the next most important feature of committees, apart from structure, is their size. The number of members will affect the working of the committee in terms of formality/informality, its methods of reaching decisions and the amount of work each member of council has to do. The larger the committee the more formal its procedures will be, the more difficult will it be to agree, and the more committees will the member have to attend. The Local Government and Housing Act 1989, implementing, as it did, many of the recommendations of the Widdicombe Report, laid down certain requirements for the composition of council committees. Where political groups are organised on a council they are obliged, in England and Wales, to apportion committee places on a basis which reflects the party political representation on the council as a whole. In practice some Scottish local authorities have adopted the same approach. This legislation was an attempt to stop the practice of a majority political group, using its majority on the council, taking all the places on a committee, particularly the powerful Policy and Resources committee (in effect creating a "cabinet" system) or "packing" other committees.

Most of the people who attend committee meetings are elected members, one of whom is the chairperson (or convener). A number of chief officers (or directors) will also be present, including the chief officer most concerned with the committee—the director of education, the director of housing, etc. There will be a committee clerk (the director of administration or his/her representative), whose responsibility it is to arrange the agenda and circulate all the relevant papers for each item of business. The committee clerk is also responsible for procedural matters and advice about some of the legal aspects of the committee's work. There will also be present the finance clerk (the director of finance or his/her representative) who is, of course, responsible for giving advice on all aspects of the financial work of the committee.

In addition to the officials mentioned in the preceding paragraph there will be present those other officials who are closely involved in the business of the committee, *e.g.* chief architect, estates surveyor, etc. These officials, or their representatives, may be present at every meeting of the committee or only on those occasions when advice is required. Some officials might only attend for one item of an agenda.

Some local authorities make it a practice to co-opt certain other non-elected members to committees. These are people who may have a particular expertise or who are representative of some area or group. Under the 1973 Act education authorities were required to co-opt representatives of religious denominations and also teacher representatives. The 1994 Act alters this. The education committee must have at least half its members as elected councillors (other committees need to have two-thirds elected councillors). The committee must still co-opt representatives of religious denominations but the requirement to have teacher representatives was abolished. This caused some controversy during the passage of the Bill but it emerged that teacher representatives can be included in the non-councillor part of the committee.

Corporate Management

In the 1960s central government departments were being restructured and streamlined to promote more efficient administration, and consequently there was pressure on local authorities to change their internal organisational structures. Both the Maud Report on the Management of Local Government (1967) and the Wheatley Report were critical of the large numbers of committees and the lack of co-ordination. The Wheatley Report endorsed the criticism of Maud in these words:

> "What is missing in local government is *unified management* . . . Some organ is needed beside the council itself in which aims can be formulated for the authority as a whole, as well as the means of achieving these aims" (para. 950).

In 1972 the Paterson Committee was set up to consider the best type of committee and management structure for the new local authorities. The structure which Paterson recommended brought to local government in Scotland two new concepts, one at committee level and at the other at officer level.

At the committee level the Paterson Report proposed a new committee called the policy and resources committee, the function of which was to include the responsibility:

> "for identifying and setting out for consideration by the whole council the fundamental objectives which the council should be aiming to achieve . . . it should have a free-ranging remit enabling it to monitor and review the performance of service committees and departments towards the attainment of the Council's objectives" (para. 4.18).

With regard to the composition of the policy and resources committee the report reviewed three options:

(a) to have a committee composed solely of the majority party—the cabinet-type system;
(b) to have minority party representation on the main committee but have a sub-committee consisting of majority party representation only;
(c) to have a multi-party committee.

However, it did not recommend any particular option, although it did say that:

"Whatever approach is adopted we stress the need to make effective arrangements for the provision of officer advice to the party groups prior to decisions being taken" (para. 4.27).

The other new aspect which the report brought to internal management was the chief executive and management team. The chief executive was not to have direct responsibility for a department in the traditional sense of the clerk's or treasurer's department but, in the larger authorities, he would have an "executive office." The role of the management team was to:

"act as the focal point for the preparation and presentation to the council, via the policy and resources committee and the service committees, of co-ordinated advice on policies, and major programmes of work" (para. 4.33).

These innovations were intended to sweep away the "excessive departmentalism" which had been seen as restricting decision-making. The type of system proposed by Paterson is usually referred to as corporate management.

Most local authorities in Scotland made changes as a result of the Paterson Report, although some of these changes were superficial. To some observers, however, changes in the management structure have only served to tilt the balance towards the officials at the expense of the elected member and the public.

The Widdicombe Report

The Paterson Report could, nowadays, be seen as a historical curiosity simply because many of the local authorities have abandoned much of what they adopted from the report. However it serves to give us a foundation upon which to understand the recommendations of the Widdicombe Report.

Relations between central and local government had not been good since the mid-1970s when restrictions on local authority finance were first introduced. By the 1980s however that relationship had further declined to, in many cases, direct confrontation. One reason for this was that many urban local authorities had become controlled by younger Labour councillors who had little time for what they saw as the "subservient" attitudes of their predecessors. Many Labour councils simply defied the Government's restrictions on finance to the brink of illegality and even past that.

After the 1983 general election the situation got worse and the Government became increasingly impatient with what it described as "extremists" in local government. One method of trying to solve the situation was adopted in England— abolition of certain local authorities. In Scotland, however, the Conservatives were alarmed at the loss to Labour of their pride and joy—Edinburgh District Council. For all the above reasons and also for party political advantage the Conservative Government in 1984 set up the Widdicombe Committee to investigate the "Conduct of Local Government Business".

The terms of reference of the committee were very wide indeed, but the main aspects of business which it was expected to cover included:

- ensuring proper accountability for decision-taking to elected members and to the electorate;
- clarifying the status and role of party groups in decision-taking;
- ensuring the proper participation and the accountability of individual elected members;
- examining any problems of propriety which may arise from members' conflicts of interests, particularly where officers of one council serve as councillors of another;
- considering the merits of the development of full-time councillors;
- reviewing the system of co-option of non-elected members;
- studying officers' relationships with elected members and political groups;
- clarifying the limits and conditions governing discretionary spending for political purposes or in relation to bodies set up by local authorities.

The committee issued an interim report in 1985 which resulted in legal restrictions on the use of public money for what the Government saw as party political propaganda. The final report of the committee was published in June 1986.

It is still difficult to assess what the Government hoped the Widdicombe Committee would do. Some commentators have suggested that the Government wanted a "respectable" excuse for further restrictions on the powers of councils and councillors. If this was the motive for the Government's action then it must have been sadly disappointed.

The committee concerned itself with the internal workings of councils and ranged its inquiry across England, Wales and Scotland. However its general tenor is that local government institutions were coping well at a time of considerable change. Although the report seemed to regret the increased politicisation of many local authorities it accepted this as a fact of life, much as the Royal Commissions before it had.

The recommendations were, therefore, based on attempting to strengthen the democratic process albeit by proposals to institute statutory codes, legally enforceable remedies and new or strengthened local government agencies. These were intended to deal with what even the committee accepted were "limited" abuses.

For Scotland the Widdicombe Committee suggested bringing local councillors more into line with their English colleagues. Scottish councillors should have to declare their intention to act within the law on taking up office. Similarly the Scottish courts should be allowed to disqualify councillors once they had been surcharged and not, as at present, on being declared bankrupt after surcharge.

For the U.K. local government system there were many other recommendations with regard to paying councillors, statutory powers for chief executives, the composition and role of policy and executive committees, the abolition of "twin tracking" (see below), increased powers for the local government ombudsman and restrictions on the rights of co-opted members.

Before anything could be done about the report another general election intervened, and it was not until 1989 that the Government got round to translating the Widdicombe recommendations into legislation. The Local Government and Housing Act 1989 applies to England, Wales and, in part, Scotland. The main provisions are:

(1) Restrictions on the political activities of senior officials. Certain staff are banned from standing as councillors. This practice stops the practice, dubbed "twin-tracking", where officials of one council were councillors on a neighbouring council. Officials cannot be councillors on their employing council and councillors cannot be employees of the council of which they are a member.

(2) Limitation of staff time off from their duties for activities such as trade union conferences.

(3) The adoption of standing orders on certain staffing matters.

(4) The requirement of councils to appoint a "monitoring officer" whose duty is to report to the council on any contravention of the law by members or staff of the council. This officer has been dubbed the "whistleblower".

(5) The right to dispose of all the housing stock if councils so wish.

The implementation of this Act was, and is, seen by many councillors as an unwarranted interference by central government in the internal affairs and management of local authorities. The assumption of the legislation is that duly elected councillors are not capable of managing their own affairs. Included in the Act was a National Code of Local Government Conduct which laid down certain conditions and standards to which councillors were expected to conform. It is ironic that it took central government another six years before it set up the Nolan Committee on Standards in Public Life and implemented some of its proposals to set Parliament's house in order.

CHAPTER 4

PUBLIC ACCOUNTABILITY

Many commentators have pointed to the growth of "big government" in recent years and it has been fashionable to talk not only of national bureaucracies but local bureaucracies as well. To many people there is a feeling of frustration when faced with the decisions of a government department or a local authority.

As a reaction to this situation there have been two trends in the political system. First, government itself has responded to demands for more participation in the decision-making process by legislating for participation or redress of grievances. Secondly, people have been organising themselves into groups in order to further some particular local cause or to reverse governmental decisions which they see as harmful to their interests. This chapter is concerned with these aspects of local government.

Community Councils

As with most of local government the Wheatley Report is a starting point for consideration of many innovations. The report was conscious of the fact that it was recommending larger local government units than had existed before. With fewer local authorities it was obvious that there would be fewer elected members. There could now be a wider gap between the electors and the elected. This possibility conflicted with the balance, which the Wheatley Commission wanted to keep, between democracy and efficiency.

Under the 1973 Act district and island authorities were given the responsibility for schemes of community councils. These schemes were required to provide for a number of items for which the local authority should ensure when community councils were set up. These items included: the areas and their boundaries; composition; methods of election; finance; and information procedures. At first there was some cynicism about community councils, partly because they were to have no statutory responsibilities and no statutory methods of raising money.

It would seem that despite the cynicism community councils, particularly in the old small burghs and rural parts of Scotland, have played an effective part in involving local people in the decision-making process of local government. Their value in the larger urban areas however may be doubted. The creation of community councils in these areas seems to be patchy. Very often the interest lies in the middle-class areas, leaving large council estates (perhaps the areas in most need of a means of pressurising local authorities) without community councils. The type of issues which community councils take up are essentially local issues mainly concerned with planning and licensing. Their mode of operation is to gather the views of local people on a particular proposal and channel these views to the local elected representatives and, if necessary, lobby the council or one of its committees.

Part of the problem, particularly in urban areas, is the existence of a number of local voluntary organisations which were in existence before community councils were set up. In this situation the local community council may have to compete for influence. Also, in terms of active personnel, there might be overlapping. It would seem, therefore, that community councils are more influential where there are no, or only weak, local voluntary organisations with which to compete.

Over the years since 1975 there seems to have been a decline in the number of community councils and, lacking statutory authority, their influence has also declined. The Government, recognising this fact, strengthened the role of community councils. Under the 1994 Act community councils were retained although local authorities have the power to revoke the existing schemes but must produce a new scheme. Provision is made for community councils to be consulted on planning and licensing matters and also the new decentralisation proposals (see below). Since many local authorities already, voluntarily, consulted community councils, and other organisations, on planning and licensing matters, the legislation only standardises the procedure.

Decentralisation

In the various reform consultation papers the Government expressed its desire to bring local government closer to the people. In its guide to decentralisation the Government suggested that there were three concepts which were essential if this idea was to work. First, it was necessary to bring services and decision-making close to the public. Secondly, to enable the public to influence and shape these services. Thirdly, to provide effective and responsive local government.

The guide suggests that there are three elements to a successful decentralisation scheme—political, managerial and physical. Political decentralisation could mean holding council and committee meetings at various locations in the area; that statutory committees like planning and education could be given a specific remit for a particular area; and that non-statutory committees could be created composed of representatives of all services in a specific area. In all of this community and voluntary organisations would play a part in a "multi-faceted dialogue".

Managerial decentralisation means that certain functions of the council may be devolved from the centre to the "point of delivery". This could be done on a functional (*e.g.* housing) or multi-service basis. The guide points out the need for staff to work across service boundaries, the need to co-ordinate services in an area and the need for staff training.

Physical decentralisation involves the provision of adequate and full information about the council's activities. This could take the form of providing a local newspaper and/or leaflets about specific activities and services of the council. Another aspect of this is to provide, what the guide calls, "one stop shops"—one office in a local authority building, *e.g.* library, in which help and guidance would be provided for all the services provided by the council.

The 1994 Act requires each council to draw up, with proper consultation, a decentralisation scheme and to submit that scheme to the Secretary of State for Scotland by April 1, 1997. The Secretary of State will not, however, approve or reject such schemes but will have to be satisfied that the statutory requirements, *e.g.* mandatory consultation with community councils, have been carried out.

Arguably, it is difficult to understand the Government's thinking on the decentralisation proposals. Such approaches were suggested in the Wheatley and Paterson Reports and many local councils have extensive and successful decentralisation schemes, notably Dundee and Edinburgh. There seems also to be an overlap with the community council schemes especially if there are to be statutory and non-statutory area committees. It may well be that the Government is seeking to extend to the whole of Scotland the "best practice" principle already in existence with regard to decentralisation.

School Councils

Unlike community councils, school councils were not suggested by the Wheatley Commission. Apart from expressing concern about the possible size of the new education authorities the Wheatley Commission, inexplicably, did not even suggest any solution to the possible "remoteness" which these larger education authorities might create.

Section 125 of the Local Government (Scotland) Act 1973 empowers local authorities to set up school and college councils but it was entirely up to the local authority to determine what, if any, functions were the responsibility of these councils. Unlike community councils there was no guidance from central government about the functions or composition of school or college councils.

The Act did not say how the composition of a school council should be set up, except to say that there should be representation of the parents, one person interested in religious education and the representatives of teaching and other staff employed in the school. For colleges the composition should be made to include "due representation of persons concerned in crafts, industries, commerce or other employments in the locality" together with representation from local interests.

As previously mentioned, the Act made no reference to the functions of school and college councils. The consequence of this was that each education authority produced its own scheme. School councils were normally based on the catchment area of a secondary school with its feeder primaries, although this could differ in some areas.

The functions of school councils also differed from area to area. Many had an "attendance" responsibility. This meant that a sub-committee was charged, in conjunction with the attendance officer, with finding reasons, from pupils, teachers and parents, for a particular pupil's poor attendance record. Most school councils had responsibility for community use of school premises outside school hours and also had some say about such items as school uniforms, school meals, extra-curricular activities, etc.

There were, however, two controversial areas where there was a clash between community involvement and professional activities. These were staff appointments and the school curriculum. Some education authorities agreed that since parents and the community had an interest in the type of staff who teach their children, there should be a parental and/or community representative present when teachers were being interviewed for a post. In some areas this was implemented only when posts like assistant head teacher were being filled. Teachers' unions have never liked this particular provision since, they argue, only a professional (*i.e.* the directorate) can judge the value of another professional.

Similarly, with the curriculum, school councils did not have the power to alter the school curriculum as decided by the head teacher and his/her staff. No doubt many school council representatives, from time to time, passed judgment on the school curriculum and many teachers were prepared to listen to the views of parents and others in this respect. However, the teachers' unions were always opposed to any interference in areas, like the curriculum, which they regarded as a professional matter.

School Boards

The above description of school councils serves two purposes. First, it provides us with a historical view of a system which was new in 1975 and which, on the whole, seemed to work reasonably well. Secondly, it provides us with a measuring rod to set against the system which the School Boards (Scotland) Act 1988 brought into existence in 1989.

In 1987 the Conservative Government issued a consultative document on school management. It was the Scottish dimension of proposals which had been implemented in England reforming the system of school governors. Both sets of proposals were based on the theory that the parents' charter proposals of 1981 should be taken a step further and that parents should be given more power over their children's education than was provided for in the existing school management system.

Whatever positive side there was to the proposals, there were some critics who saw a negative and sinister side to them. Giving more power to school boards was bound to take away powers from the education authorities and could be seen as a further erosion of local authority powers.

After receiving a considerable response to their initial proposals the Government issued another set of proposals which made some concessions to the concerns expressed. On the basis of these new proposals the Government went ahead to legislate for them in the School Boards (Scotland) Act 1988.

In essence the new system abolished school councils and replaced these with a school board for every primary, secondary and special school regardless of size, with the following features:

(1) The boards are composed of a majority of parents (up to seven) elected from the parents; up to three staff members chosen by their colleagues although these need not all be teachers; and up to three co-opted members chosen by the boards, who could be parents, staff or local representatives. Since the parents hold the majority of places it is possible that the co-opted members could be sympathetic to the elected parents.

(2) The powers of school boards are delegated to them by the local education authority.

(3) School boards are not allowed to interfere in professional issues rightly the responsibility of teachers but they are able to "give advice forcibly", in the Government's words, since they can claim that they represent the views of the parents and the local community.

(4) School boards have a role in appointing senior staff and are able to make representation to the education authority on the appointment of other staff.

Although the Government had consistently said, in the early stages of the legislation, that it was not going to give the new school boards powers to "opt-out", nevertheless legislation, the Self-Governing Schools etc. (Scotland) Act 1989, was enacted. This Act allows schools to leave the local authority education system and administer themselves. Such schools are not private schools but are directly financed by the Scottish Education Department and otherwise function on the same basis as local authority schools. This policy of the Government has, up until now, not been a success. The only schools which have attempted to "opt-out" are those which have been threatened with closure by the education authority. At the time of writing only two schools in Scotland have opted-out. It would seem that the Government seriously underestimated the loyalty of many parents in Scotland to the local authority education system.

Mention has already been made of the Parents' Charter and under this there are to be implemented certain new proposals affecting school boards. These boards have a legal role in selecting head, deputy head and assistant head teachers and they may have representatives on selection panels for other teachers. From 1996 schools are implementing "devolved school management". Under this system head teachers must consult school boards on spending decisions.

Voluntary Organisations

The 1960s saw an increase in the number of groups concerned with specific local problems. The main stimulus for this was the number of planning decisions made by local authorities, particularly with regard to redevelopment schemes and motorway construction. These decisions seemed not to have taken account of local interests and needs. It was for this reason that the Skeffington Report, *People and Planning*, was published, and subsequent legislation has made it incumbent on local authorities to publicise their planning decisions and to consult with local interests.

It was not just in the planning field that pressure groups or interest groups developed. Protests about living conditions in new mass housing schemes of high storey flats, about lack of any nursery facilities and about lack of recreational facilities, created a sort of "issue politics" at the grass roots, often concerned with the quality of the environment. Added to this in recent years is a growing number of groups concerned with conservation and with housing rehabilitation and dampness.

Local authorities have had to take more notice of these groups than central government simply because of the decisions which these local authorities have to take in the fields of planning, housing, education, etc. Very often, of course, councils and councillors have seen these pressure and interest groups as politically motivated but this type of development is not peculiar to Britain. We have had pressure and interest group politics at national level for many years but the response at local level is almost certainly due to the bureaucratisation of local government.

The role and future of voluntary community organisations at local level is probably dependent on availability of money. Some of these organisations, unlike community councils, have been powerful enough to extract money from regional and district authorities and also from the European Union. However, as local authorities cut back on expenditure this, in turn, reduces the "matching funds" which the European Union requires when it gives grants.

Local authorities have tried to cope with the problems of greater citizen participation by the appointment of various types of community social workers. The manifestation of community education programmes in Scotland is a direct result of the realisation by local authorities of the need to cater for the needs and listen to the views of groups of people with particular needs or problems.

There seems little doubt, therefore, that despite the success or otherwise of community councils, voluntary organisations at the local level who take up local issues will stay as part of the local government scene. Many local authorities have tried to cater for this, but whether they will continue to allocate sometimes scarce resources remains to be seen.

Local Government Ombudsman

Local groups trying to solve local problems in a collective way may be one thing, but when individuals have a personal grievance what machinery can redress this? In the 1960s central government came to realise that the complexities of its own procedures often caused people to suffer unnecessarily. There was pressure, led by MPs, to create some system which would sit in judgment on the actions of "faceless" civil servants. It was out of this pressure that the Parliamentary Commissioner for Administration—"the Ombudsman"—was created.

It is not surprising to find that the Wheatley Report discussed briefly the arguments for and against the setting up of a local government system for redress of grievances. No recommendation was made but the Local Government (Scotland) Act 1975 (not the 1973 Act) set up the office of Commissioner for Local Administration in Scotland. The aim of this machinery was to give members of the public who felt that they had sustained injustice as a result of maladministration by any local authority (or joint board) the same right to have their complaints independently scrutinised as they have through the Parliamentary Commissioner for Administration.

The Commissioner for Local Administration in Scotland is appointed by the Secretary of State for Scotland in consultation with the local authorities. He has two functions laid down by statute: first, to publish an annual report on the complaints investigated each year and the outcome of these investigations; secondly, to keep under review the machinery for investigating complaints and recommending any necessary changes.

The authorities whose activities are subject to investigation are the following:

- the unitary and island authorities
- committees, joint committees or boards with members appointed by local authorities

Where a local authority delegates its powers to a particular body the actions of such bodies are liable to investigation also.

The matters which are subject to investigation are any complaint made by or on behalf of a member of the public who claims to have sustained injustice consequent upon action (or non-action) by an authority. Certain rules however are laid down concerning the procedure for such complaints. Under the 1975 Act the complaint had to be channelled through a local councillor, but the Local Government Act 1988 now allows the complainant to go directly to the Commissioner. Further, the complaint must be within 12 months of the matter, unless the Commissioner considers that it is reasonable to entertain a later complaint; the complaint must not be a matter for any court or tribunal; the complaint must be an individual complaint and not a collective complaint common to a number of people.

There is provision in the legislation for the Commissioner not to investigate the complaint if he thinks there are no grounds for this; however, he must give reasons for so deciding. If a complaint has been investigated then he must report his findings and recommendations to the parties concerned. One difficulty which has been criticised is that although the Commissioner may recommend that the complaint be remedied, there is no legal obligation on the local authority so to do. However it is up to the councillors, not the council officials, to decide what action, if any, should be taken.

The undernoted statistics give some indication of the scale and nature of the complaints referred to and pursued by the Commissioner in 1994–95:

Number of cases referred	1,002
Number of cases pursued	556

Nature of those pursued:

Housing	33%
Planning	18%
Land/property	10%
Finance	7%
Miscellaneous	32%

The numbers have changed as the role and scope of the Commissioner has changed over the years. Previously, complaints had to be channelled through a councillor. Now complaints are referred directly to the Commissioner. If the complaint can be remedied before investigation so much the better. If it cannot then it is investigated. The Labour Party has indicated that it will review the role of the Ombudsman.

CHAPTER 5

EXPENDITURE

Local government finance has always been controversial. Since the nineteenth century local authorities have had to look to central government to finance some of the local services. After the Second World War it was the policy of all governments to lay down standards for services, and they had to supply taxpayers' money to ensure that local authorities maintained these standards.

In this sense local authorities have become more dependent on central government and the consequence of this has been that central government has used local authority expenditure as one of a number of economic weapons in pursuit of whatever is the current financial philosophy. This has meant that local authorities have had to change their financial procedures to cope with these new circumstances.

Much of this chapter is taken up with describing the traditional procedures used by local authorities, the methods by which central government has attempted to control local authority expenditure and the reactions by local authorities to these controls.

Financial Accounts

There is hardly any need to stress the importance of local government finance. Indeed it was argued at the time when the Royal Commissions were set up in 1966 that it was a grave omission that they should not investigate finance. It was argued also that, if anything was wrong with local government, it was because of the finance available, or not available, to the local authorities and therefore looking at structure was a cosmetic job where the root cause of the problems of local government was money.

This section will concern itself with current practice in financial procedures. By the nature of it, these procedures are

63

complex and at times detailed, but have been built up over many years. Changes are difficult to make, even where the ideas of corporate management have been implemented.

Many of the procedures which local authorities adopt for expenditure are forced upon them by central government. For instance, although it is usual practice in terms of expenditure to keep separate capital and revenue accounts, over many years central government has insisted that the local authorities keep separate housing accounts—both capital and revenue. Each of these accounts will be explained in the next few paragraphs.

Leaving aside the peculiar nature of housing accounts, "capital" and "revenue" have a particular meaning in local government. Broadly speaking, expenditure of a capital nature covers items which have a lasting value, although the value may diminish (depreciate) in time. The largest group of items of this nature would be the "bricks and mortar" of the authority—schools, halls, sports centres, roads, sewers, together with the necessary land.

However, this definition of capital leaves a lot of room for interpretation. It is easy to assume that large items are capital items, but there are many small items which also have lasting value—yet one authority may put these under "revenue" and another authority may put them under "capital".

Examples of these would include cars and vans, microcomputers and maintenance equipment. Indeed it is because there are considerable "grey areas" between capital and revenue items that some local authorities have been able to exercise "creative accountancy".

Essentially revenue items are the non-permanent or consumable elements of the authority's expenditure and include wages and salaries, heating and lighting, insurance, normal property and maintenance costs and supplies (like cleaning materials, food, etc.).

The division between capital and revenue is not just an academic distinction—it is vitally important in determining how such expenditure is to be financed. Because it has the power to borrow money for capital items, a local authority can spread the cost of these items over the assumed life of the asset, thus reducing the immediate impact on expenditure. In contrast, it meets the cost of revenue expenditure in the years in which it was incurred and cannot borrow in the long term to meet this expenditure.

In practice local authorities keep a number of different accounts, partly because of legislation, *e.g.* housing accounts, and partly because of accounting practice. However all local authorities must have a general fund and a consolidated loans fund.

Housing Accounts

Although this chapter is concerned primarily with expenditure, nevertheless this may be a good place to consider the special nature of housing accounts—both expenditure and income. Local authorities are obliged to keep these accounts separate. It is not possible to transfer income or expediture between housing and general services accounts in the same manner that transfers can be made between general services accounts.

Let us take housing expenditure first. The main expenditure in this account is on the building of new houses, the rehabilitation of older houses and capital maintenance and repair, *i.e.* repairs, like new roofs, which are needed to the structure of the building. As indicated in Chapter 2, there has been a decline in new council house building.

On the income side of the housing capital account is money borrowed, which is subject to government limits and controls, and receipts from the sale of council houses. In the early 1980s many Labour authorities were loth to sell council houses and found excuses for dragging their feet. The Government responded by increasing the discount to sitting tenants, thereby increasing the potential sales, and then linking sales receipts to new housing investment. The irony of the present situation is that the more the council sells its houses the more money it has for housing investment and these same Labour councils are now actively, if reluctantly, selling houses.

The Housing Revenue Account (HRA) has been the main area for change and controversy in the last few years. Included under the heading of HRA expenditure is repayment of capital, interest charges, regular repair and maintenence, management, council tax and loss of rent. Each of these expenditure heads has to be explained.

Capital repayment and interest charges are in historic terms which means, since capital borrowing for houses is usually on a 60 year term, that the council is still repaying capital and interest on houses which it has sold. Council house building only started in earnest in the 1920s. As indicated earlier, maintenance costs have risen in recent years, once again because of sales. It tends to be the better maintained houses in better areas that get sold thus leaving older and poorer houses which require more maintenance.

It may seem surprising that councils are required to pay a proportion of the council tax for their own property but legislation demands that "void" houses—those presently with no tenants—are assumed to have a tenant and, as landlord, the council is obliged to pay a proportion of the charge for this notional tenant. Finally, it is obvious that as houses are sold there will be a loss of rent and this has to be taken account of in expenditure. Also there will be loss of rent where tenants fail to pay and the amount has to be written off. In this respect many factors contribute to this loss. Obviously as rents rise there will be more difficulties in paying rent. Some local authorities have blamed the government's housing benefit scheme, since it is so complicated that many previous recipients are not claiming and, therefore, have less income to pay rent.

Included under the heading of HRA income is rents, housing support grant (if any) and agency fees. Each of these has to be explained. Rents now constitute 95 per cent of income on HRA, a figure which has risen steadily over the years because of the Government's policy of trying to make housing self-financing. Housing support grant is the government's contribution to housing which parallels the revenue support grant (see later). This has been steadily reduced so that, at present, only a few local authorities in Scotland qualify for this grant.

Many local authorities act as agents for service providers. They may, for instance, install and maintain gas or electric heating systems and charge the respective company a fee for this service.

Until 1988 local authorities were able to "subsidise" HRA from the general service account. This was a method of keeping rents down and, incidentally, reducing the aggregate amount of unpaid rent. However, since that date, it has not been possible for local authorities to do this and, consequently, the rents of council houses has steadily risen.

Budgetary Procedures

Although some local authorities took the opportunity to implement new budgetary procedures, it must be admitted that few local authorities changed their procedures in any radical way. This is not to say that traditional approaches have been retained, but such changes as have taken place have been in response to outside, mainly central government, pressures rather than any desire from within the authorities to change procedures. Some tried the new systems but reverted to the old practices.

Financial procedures in a local authority inevitably centre round the annual budget. Whatever procedures, new or old, are adopted by a local authority, there is a statutory requirement to fix the council tax during the month of March. The traditional method of proceeding with an annual budget was for each department of the authority to calculate its costs for its ongoing activities—in other words, to assume the service would continue at the same pace as in the previous year. Added to this would be the costs incurred in creating new services or developing or expanding existing services.

These departmental estimates would then be submitted to the appropriate committee for their approval or amendment. The estimates would then go from the service committees to the Director of Finance, who would aggregate the various estimates, add amounts for inflation and contingencies, deduct estimated revenue grants and then calculate the rate poundage (now Band D, the Scottish average) council tax amount. These provisional estimates would then go to the finance committee, who would review the aggregate amounts and, if they regarded the amounts as too high, refer all or some of the departmental estimates back to the service committees.

In recent years this traditional budgeting system has undergone considerable changes. These changes have been the result of the implementation of corporate management, and, more importantly, the imposition of strict spending guidelines by central government. The traditional system has had to take account of the implementation of cash limits by central government. This method of controlling local authority expenditure (capital and revenue) forced local authorities to adopt a system which, effectively, turned the traditional system on its head.

As explained above, the traditional procedure was for service committees to calculate their own estimates and process these through the finance committee (or sub-committee). The total estimates (normally trimmed by the finance committee) were simply all the service committee estimates added up. Cash limits, however, entailed the central government and/or the finance (or policy) committee deciding beforehand what the total expenditure should be and then indicating to the service committee their share of this total. The committee then had discretion as to how they spent their share. Additional expenditure required later would have to get approval from the policy committee.

The cash limit system was imposed by central government as a response to the economic difficulties of the mid-1970s and was tightened under the financial controls of the Conservative Government in the 1980s and 1990s. Many local authorities chose to adopt this system in any event because it strengthened the corporate management process and allowed local authorities to consider resource allocation. However it would be wrong to suggest that cash limits resulted in a widespread discussion of the objectives of local authorities or the objectives of particular local government services.

Financial Control

The calculation of estimates and the control of expenditure is largely the task of the director of finance and the finance department. By its very nature the finance department will involve a great deal of specialist knowledge and work. Finance departments, nevertheless, will vary from authority to authority but, generally speaking, will be involved in the following tasks:

- all matters pertaining to estimates;
- control of expenditure;
- internal and external audit;
- payment of accounts and collection of income;
- review of charges;
- investment of funds;
- banking and insurance arrangements;
- borrowing;
- pay control.

As far as internal audit is concerned, the Chartered Institute of Public Finance and Accountancy (CIPFA) have attempted to lay down standard principles and practices which suggest that the objectives of internal audit should be:

(1) a system of control;
(2) the improvement and continuous review of controls and procedures;

(3) continuous examination to eliminate fraud, waste, and irregular expenditure; and
(4) monitoring the use of resources.

As can be seen, internal audit has become a wider exercise than mere financial control, and many observers have felt that this function should be transferred from the director of finance's department to the chief executive's office, particularly that part of internal audit dealing with performance review. However, there are many disadvantages to this move—not least that it might weaken the ability of the finance department to keep a continuous check on financial matters.

The Local Government (Scotland) Act 1973 lays down the functions of the Commission for Local Authority Accounts in Scotland—the Accounts Commission. Under section 97(2) of that Act these functions include: (a) securing the audit of all accounts of local authorities; (b) advising the Secretary of State on any matter relating to the accounting of local authorities which he may refer to them for advice. This form of external audit was an innovation for local authorities and has created some criticism about interference in local authority decision-making. The reason for this criticism is the method by which the Accounts Commission carries out its remit.

The Controller of Audit, who is the chief official, issues particular reports on his observations of local authority accounts. He can issue special "malpractices" reports under the 1973 Act (see also Chapter 3, under Councillors). There is a statutory requirement by the Commission to present an annual report to Parliament. The views in this annual report are usually based on specific reports by auditors about general practices (or problems of procedure) adopted by individual local authorities.

The individual auditor's reports to local authorities contain advice about the organisation of an authority's financial affairs. Some local authorities see this as widening the scope of audit into the efficiency field and involving political judgments which auditors should not be involved in. The Commission claims that it (and the various auditors) are simply carrying out the will of Parliament as expressed in legislation.

The Local Government Act 1988 extended the powers of the Accounts Commission. This legislation lays a duty on the

Commission to undertake studies of local authorities with the aim of getting better value for money (VFM). One aspect of VFM has been "performance indicators" (PIs). However this approach, *i.e.* to measure the performance of services, has not been successful mainly because many local authorities do not have staff dealing with this specifically. Although many local authorities have statements of objectives the system is often ignored in the budget procedures. There are many other aspects of VFM which remind one of the corporate management system of the 1970s but it is unreasonable to insist on local authorities implementing new financial control mechanisms while, at the same time, limiting and controlling their expenditure.

Central Government Controls

As indicated earlier, all governments over the last two decades have been pursuing restraint on public expenditure. Local authorities' expenditure amounts to almost a third of total public expenditure and, therefore, what local authorities do is important to government policies.

The machinery for what has been called "macro-economic management" has become very sophisticated in recent years. The most general control which the government has is the Public Expenditure Survey. This sets out annually proposals for future expenditure in the short and medium terms but it is not mandatory on local authorities. The survey simply indicates to the local authorities what the government's priorities are over a period of two or three years. It does, however, give the authorities a clue about the possible nature of the other controls wielded by government.

The second control which the government uses is that over capital investment. This is sometimes referred to as capital allocation and it has two features. First, it can apply to a service, *e.g.* education or housing, where the government indicates the maximum total amount it expects all local authorities to spend on capital projects within the particular service. Secondly, as far as individual local authorities are concerned, each is given a maximum net capital allocation. This may be enhanced by raising capital receipts through the sale of land and property. This gross capital allocation is the maximum amount the local authority is allowed to *spend* in the year. To the central government the *sources* of capital finance (borrowing, capital grants, capital receipts or out of revenue) are immaterial since the central government is here concerned with capital investment and balancing this between the public and private sectors of the economy.

From time to time, the government will issue supplementary capital allocations, *e.g.* to deal with winter emergencies. These (like the annual capital allocations) are issued in terms of section 94 of the 1973 Act. Here the central government is saying to the local authority that it is allowing the local authority to spend its own money on a particular project.

Of course the government has other methods of controlling capital expenditure by local authorities. About a third of all capital borrowed by local authorities is borrowed from the Public Works Loan Board. The board gets its funds directly from the government (authorised by Parliament) and therefore it is possible for the government to limit the amount available to the board, thus restricting the local authorities' sources of borrowing. The government can also restrict the quota which local authorities are allowed to borrow from the board. This quota varies according to need and total outstanding debt. Borrowing from the board is discussed further in Chapter 6.

Through the Bank of England the central government can influence the banks' lending rates, and thus whatever sources local authorities have for borrowing money the market rate can be influenced by government. The level of the rate of interest is a major consideration to a local authority about to borrow for capital projects, since the interest paid is financed out of the revenue account. By increasing interest rates, therefore, the central government indirectly deters any local authorities from borrowing.

The government also controls the revenue expenditure of local authorities but since this is mainly done indirectly by restricting the authorities' income from grants, charges and taxes, these will be dealt with in Chapter 6.

CHAPTER 6

SOURCES OF FINANCE

The other side of the book-keeping exercise from expenditure is obviously income. Local authority income derives from many sources nowadays but, like expenditure, is broken into capital and revenue income. Although sources of capital have not changed much in recent years the sources of revenue income have undergone major changes which have had considerable political repercussions. We shall deal with capital first because it is the easier to understand and is organised on a longer-term basis than revenue income.

Sources of Capital

Local authorities mostly borrow money for capital projects and items. The Local Government (Scotland) Act 1975 provides the main powers for local authorities to borrow money. Under this Act they may raise money in a number of ways—mortgages, stock, annuity certificates, bonds, bills or other means approved by the Secretary of State, and they also have powers to raise money outside the United Kingdom. In practice, however, borrowing money is very strictly controlled by central government as indicated in the previous chapter.

Of the sources of capital finance mentioned above, the largest proportion is borrowed from the Public Works Loan Board. The Public Works Loan Board lends money to local authorities and other public agencies. The board is financed by government loans and the rate of interest is prescribed by the Treasury. There is little need to go into the rather complicated procedures used by the board to lend money to local authorities.

Two aspects of the board are important, however. First, local authorities can only borrow so much from the Public

Works Loan Board—"the quota", which is equal to a proportion of the local authorities' outstanding debt or annual
capital payments. This quota can be varied by the Treasury,
depending on the government's financial policies. In addition, the government could deter the local authorities from
borrowing from the Public Works Loan Board—thus forcing
them into the market. Secondly, since the rate of interest is
ultimately controlled by the government, again the government can control the level of local authority borrowing from
the Public Works Loan Board.

Nevertheless, there are some advantages in borrowing
from this source. Principally, the Public Works Loan Board
can be used where other sources of borrowing may be
difficult for a local authority, and secondly, the borrowing
arrangements are a little more flexible than in the open
market. The Public Works Loan Board can also act as a lender
of last resort outwith the quota mentioned above—but at a
cost.

As mentioned above, local authorities are allowed to borrow money from sources outside the United Kingdom, but
this is very strictly controlled by the Treasury and the Bank of
England. This mainly means the institutions of the European
Union. For instance, loans are available for the following
categories of expenditure:

    (a) creation of employment in areas of declining
        industries;
    (b) industrial estates and the restoration of derelict land;
        and
    (c) certain specific projects in under-developed regions.

In addition to borrowing for capital projects, both the
United Kingdom Government and the European Union will
give grants to local authorities for specific projects. The trend
in recent years, by the Government, has been to provide
grants in conjunction with other public agencies. For instance,
many infrastructure projects (roads, urban renewal) received
grants from the Scottish Industry Department and Scottish
Enterprise (formerly the Scottish Development Agency).
Again, the European Union will give grants for specific
projects in agriculture, fishing, retraining, job creation and job
maintenance schemes.

The controls which central government has exercised over
local authority capital expenditure have varied over the
years. The current procedure is that local authorities submit a
five-year capital programme to central government. Central

government then informs local authorities of their capital allocation—this is the maximum amount which a local authority will be allowed to spend in the next financial year. Within this allocation there are limits to capital spending set for specific services. It must be stressed that capital allocation is not money which the central government gives to local authorities (that would be a grant)—it is the amount local authorities are allowed to spend, no matter how they get that money.

As restrictions on capital expenditure tightened in the early 1980s, particularly in housing, many local authorities tried to find loopholes in the law. This became known as "creative accountancy". It has to be pointed out here that capital spending restrictions were not subject to the same financial penalties as revenue spending restrictions simply because sources of borrowing were not directly controlled by central government.

One method of getting round capital allocations was for local authorities to lease capital items rather than borrow money for them. A variation of this was for local authorities to sell a capital item and then "lease-back". Thus buildings, land or equipment could be sold off, the money used for capital projects and the item leased back from the buyer. This was a method more commonly used by English local authorities. The consequence of this, however, was that the leasing payments had to come out of revenue accounts. The Government closed this loophole and since March 1987 new lease-back arrangements have not been allowed.

Another method of getting round the restriction was for local authorities to raise money by "covenant". Basically this meant that local authorities borrowed money from, mainly overseas, banks on a medium term loan at rates of interest higher than the market rate. These loans would be for a specific purpose, often housing, and the capital item would serve as collateral for the loan. The end result of this was to defer payment of the loan over a long period of time and add to revenue expenditure for a long time into the future.

Once again the Government acted to close this loophole. Local authorities who financed capital by covenant now find that, although they may have money to spend in the short term, the Government reduces their capital allocation in the long term. Over a period of time, therefore, their average capital expenditure has to match what it would have been if the covenants had not been taken out.

It would be wrong to complete an explanation about capital finance without mentioning that new capital borrowing does not occupy a large amount of a finance department's time. Most of the work is concerned with servicing ongoing loans. This can involve the re-financing of existing loans and the management of long-term and temporary borrowing. New capital expenditure amounts to less than a fifth of existing debt.

Sources of Revenue

Turning now to revenue income, this requires some detailed explanation. Local authorities derive their income from three general sources—the council tax, the business rates and the revenue support grant. In addition specific services like social work, recreation, education, etc., generate income from charges for all or part of the service. These charges, however, are designated to the specific service and deducted from the gross expenditure for that service (department). The total net expenditure for the local authority, *i.e.* the sum of each department's net expenditure, is met from the council tax, business rates and the revenue support grant.

A major source of local authority income is the revenue support grant which pays for over 80 per cent of aggregate local authority net spending in Scotland. The calculation of the RSG is complicated and has changed significantly in the last few years.

The global amount of revenue support grant is determined by the government in accordance with the estimates of relevant expenditure by the local authorities. What is "relevant expenditure" is defined by legislation, but includes most of the local authority services except those which receive a specific grant like the police, urban aid or housing.

However, instead of distributing the RSG on a simple headcount basis, a number of factors are taken into account. Part of the calculation takes into account the particular needs of an area. For example, a local authority which has more than the (Scottish) average of school children or old people per head of population will have to devote more of its resources to these groups. Therefore these groups (called client groups) are "weighted" in the calculation.

As mentioned previously, housing finance is kept separate from other (general services) finance. The system of distribution of support for housing (the housing support grant) is also very complex, but has been phased out almost completely now.

In addition to the above grants, local authorities can receive specific grants. Both central government and other public agencies can give them. Examples of these are the specific grants which central government gives for police services, community care, urban renewal, etc. Other public agencies, like the Arts Council, the Sports Council, etc., are empowered to give grants for a specific service or project.

The Community Charge

The origins of the community charge (poll tax) lie back in the 1960s. Concern about the level of local authority spending was one element in the setting up of the two Royal Commissions of 1966–69. Both of these commissions, however, excluded a review of local government finance. The government of the day felt that the time to consider finance was after the commissions had reported.

In 1971 the Conservative Government issued a green paper, *The Future Shape of Local Government Finance*, in which it set out a number of advantages and disadvantages of a number of alternatives to replace the rating system. Although there was considerable discussion at the time, no further action was taken. After local government reform in 1973–74 there was a considerable rise in the level of rates, sparking off much criticism and protest which the newspapers of the day described as a "ratepayers' revolt". The two main political parties were forced to take account of this in the general elections of 1974. The Conservatives pledged that they would do away with the system and the newly returned Labour government set up an inquiry—the Layfield Committee.

The Layfield Report, published in 1976, was a very exhaustive study of local government finance and still remains a valuable source of statistics for those interested in the subject. The recommendations, however, are of little value now, although it is worth noting that the committee suggested that local income tax should be explored as a *supplement* to local rating and that valuation of property should shift from rental values to capital values.

As with the 1971 green paper, nothing was done about the Layfield proposals until the Conservative Government issued another green paper in 1981, *Alternatives to Domestic Rates*. The message of this document was that there was no viable alternative to the rating system although a variety of supplements could be made to work. By 1983 it seemed that the rating system devised in the nineteenth century was going to remain stubbornly durable.

However events were to bring the issue to crisis point. One of the main criticisms of the rating system was that there were not enough revaluations of property to keep pace with inflation. Valuations were supposed to take place every five years but because of their unpopularity all governments had found excuses for delay or postponement. Scotland was due to have a revaluation in 1985 (the previous revaluation had been 1977) and England and Wales had not had a revaluation since 1973.

Inevitably after long periods between revaluations rental values leapt considerably (up to three times in 1985) and ratepayers became alarmed. The Conservative Government responded to this alarm by announcing it would carry out its election pledge (of 1979) to abolish domestic rating. The problem was what to replace it with? To most people's surprise they proposed to replace domestic rates with a "poll tax", a flat rate tax on adults, which was to be named the community charge. This type of tax had never been seriously considered by the parade of inquiries and green papers since the 1970s. Indeed the Government itself had dismissed the idea in 1983.

Nevertheless in 1986 the Government's proposals were published in a document *Paying for Local Government*. There was to be legislation for the new tax first in Scotland and then, eventually, in England and Wales. In pursuance of these proposals the Abolition of Domestic Rates etc. (Scotland) Act 1987 was passed just before the 1987 general election.

From April 1989 in Scotland domestic rates were abolished and replaced by a community charge. Popularly known as the poll tax, this was a flat rate charge levied on all adults within an area. In addition the old water rate was replaced by a water charge which was added to the community charge. A rebate system existed for certain categories of adults. The 1987 Act also reformed the non-domestic rates, *i.e.* rates paid by commercial and public bodies. Henceforth non-domestic rates were decided, not by the local authorities, but by the Secretary of State for Scotland. The ultimate aim of this reform was to bring non-domestic rates, eventually, into line with those in England and Wales. A transitional programme was developed so that by 1995 non-domestic rates would be a national (*i.e.* United Kingdom wide) tax and this was renamed the business rate.

From its inception the community charge caused administrative problems. A separate community charge register had to be compiled. There was a misconception (or suspicion) by many people that the Electoral Register and the Community Charge Register were linked and those people who wished to avoid paying the community charge simply did not register for either. There were many problems associated with the rebate and collection systems. Many Scottish local authorities were opposed to the new system and simply dragged their feet on implementation.

The opposition parties waged a campaign against the new tax although this was always within the law. However, there were others, individuals (councillors and MPs) and groups, who campaigned for non-payment. Over the four years of its existence (1989–1993) these campaigns resulted in massive arrears of income to local authorities amounting, at one point, to as much as 30 per cent of income. Since the community charge was associated with Mrs Thatcher it was no surprise that with the new administration under Mr Major the system (which was, in some cases, violently opposed in England) would be reviewed. This resulted in the abolition of the community charge and its replacement by the council tax.

The Council Tax

In one sense the council tax could be described as a compromise between domestic rates and the community charge. It is essentially a property tax. The new tax is based on households which receive one bill thus obviating the need for a register of individuals. The amount to be paid is based on two elements—the capital value of the property occupied and the number of adults in the household. A single adult receives a 25 per cent discount; if there is no one resident in the property there is a 50 per cent discount. If there are more than two adults in the household the tax rate is increased. The property element of the tax is important. Property is divided into eight bands based on capital value (not rental value as in the old rates). There is a separate water and sewerage charge which is now levied by the three water authorities but is collected, in the meantime, by the local authorities.

Thus the tax is both a property tax and a personal tax but, unlike the community charge, it does take account of personal circumstances and, therefore, can be described as a "progressive" tax like income tax. Secondly, it is much easier to administer and collect than the community charge. Thirdly, and this was the cornerstone of the Government's reform programme since 1986, it is paid by a large proportion of the adult population and thus makes local authorities more "accountable" compared with the less than half of the adult population who paid domestic rates. This latter circumstance, in the Government's view, led to local authority profligacy.

The Secretary of State has the power to impose a limit, or "cap", on the maximum amount that a local authority can charge. This contentions power, strongly opposed by COSLA, has been used against several local authorities in Scotland.

The fact that there has been no campaign against the tax and that local authorities have accepted it suggests that it is an improvement on the community charge. But the political consequences of the community charge have been significant if the national opinion polls and the local government elections are any indicator, with the Conservatives continuing to decline. It may take some time for the Conservatives to live down their association with the very unpopular community charge.

CHAPTER 7

A FUTURE FOR LOCAL GOVERNMENT?

The previous chapters on local government history, functions and finance have touched on various features of central government control. How these controls have developed is, in many ways, a contemporary history of local government. Since it is central government that chooses when to introduce new legislative controls and how to implement them it is necessary to look at the aims and objectives of the Government to try to discern the future role of local government.

It is essential to remember the way in which local government is empowered to act in order to appreciate the full extent to which the Government could go if it was determined to make major changes.

Local authorities derive their powers, duties and responsibilities from Acts of Parliament. The important principle of *ultra vires,* strictly applied, means that local authorities can only undertake activities which are specially approved by Parliament. These Acts, nevertheless, allow for considerable variation in discretion left with the local authorities.

Statutory powers enacted for local authorities vary widely in terms of discretion. At one end of the spectrum local authorities have no room for variation. Such items as electoral registration or housing benefit leave little or no power of discretion to the local authorities. The regulations must be carried out to the last detail. However, at the other end of the spectrum local authorities can be given general powers to deal with, for example, libraries or swimming baths in whatever way they think necessary.

In essence, therefore, local authority legislation confers powers rather than duties. It was for this reason that it was possible for local authorities to challenge the right of central government control. If a central government department could not point to statutory provisions authorising intervention then it could not intervene, although it could use other means of persuasion like reduction of grant or delay of approval.

The Consequences of Reform

Government policy and consequent legislation from the 1980s, however, has tended to turn powers into duties. This has meant that where an authority had discretionary powers to do, or not do, something, new legislation has defined specifically that an authority must do, or must not do, something. Examples of this are instructive. Whereas, in the past, local authorities had power to decide whether contracts for a particular service could be given to outside contractors, they are now, by legislation, obliged to offer the contract to any bidder. Irrespective of the rights and wrongs of this system the fact of the matter is that local discretion has given way to obligation.

Another example of this trend is in housing. In the past local authorities were always free to sell council houses. Now they are obliged to do this if the tenant so wishes. But the tenant's wish is determined by the large discount allowed. That discount is determined by central government and not by the local authority. Similarly, under the self-governing schools legislation, schools are allowed to opt-out of the local authority education system if the school board so votes. Although this has not happened much in Scotland it does not alter the fact that the local authority has no option but to concede if the school board so wishes to opt-out. One final example is the legislation which allows the Secretary of State for Scotland to determine the level of the business rate, thus replacing the previous right of the local authority to determine this.

The above remarks illustrate the relationship now between central and local government. In the past that was a working relationship where the central government allowed local authorities to run their area according to the mandate they received from the local electorate so long as it conformed to certain national guidelines which ensured that standards would not fall below a certain national minimum. Now the situation is that local authorities appear to be the administrative arm of central government and the veneer of local elections is precisely that, a veneer, an illusion that there is "local democracy". This situation also erodes the right of the local electorate to exercise its political right to choose, or throw out, the local administration.

Throughout the 1980s and 1990s the Conservatives were in a weak electoral position in Scottish local government. The Labour Party controlled the "big" regions and dominated COSLA. Nevertheless by the mid 1990s local authorites were losing powers. They only directly controlled about 15 per cent of their income and had witnessed increasing government control and "creeping" privatisation through the CCT system. Effectively the Conservatives controlled local government simply by centralising it. Changes in the powers and effectiveness of local authorities allowed the Conservatives to promote the idea that there was need of a "slimmed down" local government system.

Encouraged by the results of the 1992 general election where the Conservatives had done better than expected the Government went ahead to propose reforms. Accusations of legislating for political advantage are harsh although there was suspicion that certain new boundaries were "doctored". The fact is that the opposition parties were not totally opposed to a reformed system—they just did not want a Conservative reformed system. In any case had the Conservatives been legislating for "gerrymandering" this was to backfire on them with the results of the 1995 local elections. There were better (Conservative) reasons for reform.

Forward to the Past?

Conservative philosophy about local government has been clear for decades. They believed that local government was inefficient hence the various reforms to finance, powers and "local monopolies". Having reformed these areas it followed that local government powers had been reduced either by increased central government control or by local competition. There seemed, now, to be no justification for "big" local authorities (especially if they were Labour controlled like Strathclyde and Lothian). To the Conservatives, therefore, if good administrative reasons for reform produced a favourable political result then this was a bonus.

Previous reforms of local government have reduced the number of local authorities—but to ever larger authorities, *e.g.* 1929 and 1975. The 1994 reform further reduced the number of local authorities but had an unusual result. It did not abolish large (in area) local authorities—Highlands,

Dumfries and Galloway, Fife and Borders still exist and with added powers—housing, recreation, etc. On the other hand it did abolish other larger authorities—Strathclyde, Central, Tayside, Grampian and Lothian and increased the powers of the old district councils—education, social work, etc. The reform, therefore, is not in the normal development, or progression, of local government reorganisation being more a rationalisation to create a single tier system. The irony of this approach is that this solution was rejected by the Wheatley Report and by the Conservative Government of 1981 after the Stodart rejection of single tier authorities. It is a rejection of the Wheatley approach (accepted on the whole by the Conservatives in 1969) that "bigger was better"—and more efficient. Why the change of approach? It seems to be the result of the Thatcher ideology of reducing the power of the state—"rolling back the state"—both at national and local level.

One aspect of the 1929 system which was highlighted by the Paterson Report was the number of committees and sub-committees in local authorities. To Paterson this resulted in inefficient decision-making with too much time spent on detail and too little time spent on long term planning. It was for this reason that Paterson recommended fewer committees and an "overseeing" committee—the policy and resources committee. With an accent on longer term planning of resources and services it was felt that the idea of annual elections (albeit for one third of the council) and three year terms for councillors was not suitable.

It is as well to remind ourselves of the above components of the Wheatley and Paterson reports because the new system, both by design and by accident, seems to be going back to the 1929 system. Wheatley argued that services should be provided in areas appropriate to the importance (and cost) of the service. Thus education, structure planning and transportation should be on a regional basis while more "community based" services like recreation and environmental services should be on a district basis. The 1994 reform rejects this. Similarly the system introduced by the 1994 Act, at the time of writing, has rejected the Paterson approach. The Conservative Government in 1995 criticised the new unitary authorities for the number of committees which they had created albeit that the Government saw it as a conspiracy to give councillors more special responsibility allowances. It remains to be seen if this "forward to the past" approach will result in more efficient decision making.

Results of the 1994 Reform

Another problem resulting from the reorganisation is the fragmentation of regional services where regional authorities have been abolished. Whatever the pros and cons of larger authorities it could be argued that, in respect of some services, regionalisation had positive results. In the transportation sector alone there can be little doubt that the provision of transport services (buses and trains) in areas like Strathclyde, Lothian, Central, Tayside, Fife and Grampian saw improvements in services. If there were criticisms in this sector it was due to the deregulation of bus services rather than bad local authority control.

It remains to be seen if the fragmentation of this provision from 1996 will result in continued benefits. There will also be a reduction of local authority subsidies to transport services particularly in respect of rural services and also to vulnerable groups like old age pensioners (concessionary fares) as the smaller authorities find that they cannot continue the level of subsidy which was made available by the regional authorities and was the result of economies of scale.

Similarly in transport the building and maintenance of major trunk roads may well suffer. There can be little doubt that the planning and provision of a regional network of roads benefited both the business community and individuals. Once again economies of scale will be difficult to sustain unless neighbouring authorities can co-operate. This co-operation may not be possible where these neighbouring authorities are of a different political complexion or where old rivalries exist. In terms of road building it would seem that the only winner is the Scottish Office, which took over the responsibility for trunk roads in the 1994 Act, leaving the local authorities with only peripheral responsibilities in this service.

Another service which may also suffer from "de-regionalisation", or "disaggregation" as it has been called, is education. Once again economies of scale provided benefits under the 1973 system. Under this system local education authorities were able to provide specialised services for students in terms of the handicapped, the specially gifted, remedial services and peripatetic teachers. Added to this was extra-curricular activities including outdoor education. It is doubtful if the new, smaller, authorities will be able to provide the same level of service.

A further difficulty may also arise with CCT. Some services like road maintenance and school meals were provided by region-wide DSOs which often won tenders because of their size and experience. Once again, only if neighbouring authorities can co-operate to continue the DSOs will the scale and quality of these provisions be continued. At the time of writing the existing road maintenance DSOs have won some major contracts despite the dislike of the Conservative Government for this type of organisation. Another aspect of this is that if the region-wide DSOs do not continue the contracts will be smaller and, therefore, less attractive to the private sector. It is doubtful if the Conservative Government's pursuit of "smaller is better" anticipated this consequence of reform.

The demise of the larger regional authorities has another dimension. Regions like Strathclyde and Lothian, over the years since 1975, have developed major links with the European Union. Indeed Strathclyde had a permanent presence in Brussels. These larger regional authorities, using their regional "clout", were able to extract major funding from the European Union. It is doubtful if any of the new unitary authorities, outside the cities, will be able to afford such links. In effect this means that the Scottish local authorities will have less influence in Europe at the same time as Europe is moving to develop regional organisations. The corollary of this is that the Scottish Office will be the only link with Europe.

This brings us to a consideration of COSLA. The 1973 system created a complicated structure for this organisation but it could be argued that COSLA has increased its power and influence since 1975 and that this was due, in part, to the presence of the larger regional authorities. It now represents 32 "equal" authorities and it remains to be seen whether this will now lead to 32 warring authorities which could well reduce the authority of COSLA. On the other hand the reduction of the influence of the "old" authorities in Europe may be an opportunity for COSLA to increase its influence there.

The 1994 reorganisation of Scottish local government cost money. The actual cost is a matter of dispute. The Conservative Government hired consultants to estimate the costs over a five year period but this estimate has been disputed. No matter what figure is chosen any reorganisation costs money. Such costs have to be justified by savings and such savings are difficult to estimate. In the short term it has to be admitted that changes in functions will cost money. The number of senior officials will be reduced but those losing or retiring from posts have to be compensated. Buildings also will be made "redundant" and it may well take time to find alternative uses. Costs of reorganisation seep down the system to junior staff and even to the cost of producing new logos, stationery, etc. It is difficult to understand why all this was found necessary. If local authorities were shorn of some powers then this should reduce their budgets although their administrative costs might not be proportionately reduced. However, there have been few figures produced to show that local authority administrative costs were rising before re-organisation although some figures have shown that, indeed, they were falling. The Conservative Government promised to produce a "hit list" of those authorities which had high administrative costs as a percentage of their budgets. Such figures do not measure "efficiency" at a time of reorganisa-tion and it is difficult to see the purpose of this exercise.

Another criticism of the new system is that it increased the power of the Scottish Office and of non-elected quangos. It has been pointed out that although there are about 1,300 directly elected councillors in the new system there are 5,000 non-elected, or indirectly elected, members of various quangos, joint boards and committees. This comparison is an ironic comment on the accusation levelled by the Conserva-tives in the late 1980s that, under the rating system, local authorities were undemocratic and unaccountable because those who paid for the services (the ratepayers) were a minority of the electorate.

Perhaps stung by these criticisms the Conservatives, in 1995, began to rethink their local government philosophy. It must be said, also, that this rethink was due to the debate over legislative devolution. Whatever the reasons behind the rethink a new definition of "devolution" began to appear. The opposition parties—Labour and Liberal Democrats (the SNP remain divided about devolution)—defined it as legisla-tive devolution with very modest tax raising (or lowering) powers. This definition was explained in the report of the Constitutional Convention in 1995. The Conservatives began to devise a definition which, for want of a better phrase, could be called "people devolution".

It can be argued that this new definition was simply an extension of the "chartist" idea of the Thatcher and Major years—the Parents' Charter, the Tenants' Charter, the Citizens' Charter, etc. The Conservatives believed that powers should be devolved from government to the people bypassing, in a sense, the local authorities. Manifestation of this thinking can be seen in the encouragement of housing associations, opted-out schools and the plans for decentralisation. Such thinking led to contradictions. The Parents' Charter was to allow parents to choose their children's school but Conservatives also favoured the return of selection tests and interviews for schools thus taking the decision out of the hands of the parents. Conservative thinking on the role of local government highlighted a dichotomy. If local authorities were to be less powerful why retain all the various controls which central government had amassed since the 1970s?

The answer to this question came in 1995 when the Secretary of State for Scotland, Michael Forsyth, responded to a COSLA document calling for the reduction of central government controls. The document *More Than 50 Ways to Improve Local Government* outlined 52 different controls which could be removed or relaxed. These controls, ranging from finance to licensing powers, had, mostly, come into force in recent years. It may be instructive to summarise these recommendations since it reminds us of the type of powers which local authorities have lost:

* Education—the removal of central government controls over school closures, amalgamations and catchment areas;
* Housing—councils to be given the right to bid for stock being transferred from other landlords (particularly the former New Towns);
* Roads—the responsibility for trunk roads to be devolved to local government;
* Finance—a number of proposals including the abolition of capping and the change to a capital expenditure system based on a single consent over three years;
* CCT—a move from compulsory to voluntary competitive tendering;
* Licensing—licensing boards should have the freedom to set fees locally subject to guidance from COSLA.

The Secretary of State annouced that he was prepared to consider these recommendations and that he would make an announcement early in 1996. At the time of writing no announcement had been made.

Many had worried that, with a devolved parliament in Edinburgh, local government would be subject to yet further reorganisation. However, in 1996, the Labour Party announced its approach to local government were it to form a government. This approach contained both a "carrot" and a "stick". The proposals included increased powers for the Accounts Commission to ensure the highest standard of service in local government. Nevertheless it also proposed that the Accounts Commission should be made more accountable to the public. Labour accepted that it would not be practical to dismantle the unitary authorities but proposed certain changes to give more freedom to local authorities. It is not surprising that many of these proposals repeat the recommendations of COSLA.

Given the above remarks it is obvious that the 1994 system will remain into the twenty-first century but with a change of emphasis. No one, officials or politicians, seems keen to make further extensive changes. Local government has been the victim of partisan decision making over the last 25 years and should be given a period to stabilise. The debate about Scottish devolution and also the debate about an integrated/ federated Europe will however mean that local government will continue to be important in the controversy about local democracy. The European idea of subsidiarity will also play a major part in the development of Scottish local government.

Those who would like to see local government powers stabilised and perhaps increased would prefer to see these powers entrenched in some form of written constitution or for all parties to accept the European Charter of Local Self-government. At the very least there should be a recognition that continued changes and interference in local government is not only undemocratic but confusing to the consumers of local services. Such confusion can only create cynicism and apathy in the electorate.

INDEX

Accounts Commission
    accountability, 89
    increased powers, proposal for,
        89
    powers of, 69, 70
    role of, 69
Audit
    Controller, 69
    internal, 68, 69

Building control
    function of, 28
    public safety, 28, 29
Burghs
    disappearance of, 4
    purpose of, 1
    reclassification, 3
    system, 2, 3
    system of 1929, under, 3
Bus services
    deregulation, 26
Business rate
    central government, decided by,
        9, 79

Central government
    controls,
        challenge to, 81
        decision-making, of, 3
        development of, 81
        local government finance, of,
            70, 71
        reduction, call for, 88
        local government, relationship
            with, 82
Children
    "at risk", responsibility for, 18
    education. See Education
    hearings, agency for, 33
Commissioners of supply
    landward areas, powers in, 1
    role of, 1
Committees
    co-option on, 46

Committees—*cont.*
    creation of, 44
    decision, making, 42
    number of, 84
    persons attending, 45, 46
    policy and resources, 47
    service, identification with, 45
    size of, 45
    sub-committees, 44
    system, 42, 44, 45
Community charge
    abolition, 79
    administrative problems, 79
    implementation of, 9
    Layfield Report, 77
    origins of, 77
    political consequences of, 80
    rates, replacement of, 78
    rebate system, 78
    register, 79
    replacement of rates by, 9
Community councils
    assisting, responsibility for, 7
    consultation, 54
    decline in number of, 54
    local people, involvement of, 54
    local voluntary organisations
        pre-dating, 54
    schemes of, 53, 54
Compulsory competitive tendering
    defined activities, 30
    Direct Service/Labour
        Organisations, 30, 31
    introduction of, 30
    local authority powers, loss of, 88
    region-wide DSOs, contracts won
        by, 86
Convention of Scottish Local
        Authorities
    advisory function, 34
    co-ordination of activities
        through, 13
    objectives of, 34